SELLING YOUR VALUABLES

*From Antiques to Collectibles,
Your Household Possessions
Are Worth More Than You Think*

Jeanne Siegel

Bonus Books, Inc., Chicago

© **1996 by Bonus Books, Inc.**

00   99   98   97   96   5   4   3   2   1

Library of Congress Cataloging-in-Publication Data

Siegel, Jeanne.
   Selling your valuables: from antiques to collectibles, your
household possessions are worth more than you think / Jeanne
Siegel.
       p.   cm.
   Includes bibliographical references and index.
   ISBN 1-56625-055-2 (paperback)
   1. Antiques—United States—Marketing.   2. Collectibles—
United States—Marketing.   I. Title.
NK1125.S49   1995
745.1'068'8—dc20   95-44075

Bonus Books, Inc.
160 East Illinois Street
Chicago, Illinois 60611

Cover photo by Marianne Siegel

Composition by Point West Inc., Carol Stream, IL

Printed in the United States of America

Dedicated to those who, whatever the reason,
must sell, might sell, or want to sell.
Selling smart is what this book is about.

Also for Julie, Philip, Marianne, William and Glenna Elizabeth,
who someday will have to clear out the Siegel household.

CONTENTS

ACKNOWLEDGEMENTS

Leslie Hindman Auctioneers, 215 W. Ohio Street, Chicago, IL
My appreciation to Leslie Hindman and to Bailey Davis

Skinner Incorporated, Auctioneers, Boston and Bolton, MA
357 Main Street, Bolton, MA
My thanks to Anne Trodella

Dunnings Auction Service, 755 Church Rd., Elgin, IL
Thank you, Shawn Dunning

H. Horwitz Co., 845 N. Michigan Ave., Water Tower Place,
Chicago, IL
Donald Horwitz

Angelo Tiesi, Altheimer & Gray, Chicago, IL

Ned L. Fishkin, Ltd., Carson Pirie Scott & Company
State Street, Chicago, IL

Thomas Joyce & Company, 400 N. Racine, Chicago, IL

Nevermore Books, Winnetka, IL
Richard Blakley and Sharon Morgan Blakley

McDrew Sales, Kenilworth, IL

Nathan Shedroff, Vivid Studios, 510 Third St.,
San Francisco, CA
Thank you for the Internet material

Julie Halpern—Proofreader

Cathy Juarez—for her excellent secretarial work

The purpose of this book is to advise sellers of their options. You have various choices. Since most readers will begin with the chapter dealing with general selling and then turn to particular categories, there will be some repetition. Selling is a financially challenging occupation worthy of your energy and time. The key word is *negotiation*.

GENERAL SELLING

If you don't have a fairy godmother, you may just have to take yourself to the ball. It's easier to turn rugs and silver into cash than it is to turn a pumpkin into a Corvette. Your magic wand is specific information. Possessions can be a delight, a burden, or the blocks with which to build a healthy bank account.

Acquiring things we needed, wanted or inherited, was usually pleasurable. Disposing of them can be troublesome. The treasure may become a mere object. Often when it is time to sell your "stuff," you may not know what the real treasures are. Wedding gifts, Grandma's china, your first apartment furniture, childhood books, or art bought simply for decorative purposes have changed in value from their original cost. You cannot sell effectively without knowing the present market value of your possessions.

Selling may introduce you to an entirely new experience. Most of you were consumers from an early age. Many people buy, if they have the means, on impulse. Impulse selling, giving away, or dumping, can really cost you. Selling will show you the other side of the coin. Patience must replace impulse. You will learn new skills, a new vocabulary, meet new people, and make new gains. Last year I had 90-year-old Josephine in one of my buying and selling classes. She gives us all hope, proving no one is too old to learn if they are interested.

Do you know how to use price guides? Are other persons involved in your decisions, such as family, almost exes, or creditors? Do you actually own all the objects you are considering selling? If you need help, this book can provide possible solutions for unfeathering your nest and enlarging your bank account.

You have choices when you decide to sell your

property. Do not settle for an inadequate price from a local resale shop just to get the pieces out of the house. Do not be content with less than a fair price when you sell.

Various market places to consider are the auction house, the dealer sale, the house sale, the garage sale, a personal sale, a newspaper classified ad, an in-house sale, or a mail sale. Even a pawnshop may be a consideration.

Have you a time schedule to meet? That alone may influence your decisions. Will you need a packing service? Will you need insurance? Will you need a mover?

Most objects can be sold. Obviously, fine pieces should bring better prices than those of lesser quality. If you sell many items, and do it thoughtfully, the checks will add up. Everything sold is not of museum quality. Sometimes collectibles sell better than fine pieces. It is very important to find out what you have, and then to learn its potential monetary worth. Often people do not really know what they have. Just recently, while doing an appraisal, I saw a wonderful, large, Victorian silver ice-water pitcher on a tilting stand with platform for a glass, sitting tarnished in a corner filled with plastic flowers. The owner thought it was merely an old coffee pot. She had paid a small price for it, at some sale, and did not think much about it. That's what I mean about finding out what you have. The owner knew she had a silver pot but she didn't know what it was, or its market value, or its potential worth.

Antique furniture sells, but so do 10-year-old pieces. Art glass hammers down great prices, and Depression-era glass also sells well. Your things will be purchased by people with various needs, interests, and resources. The trick is to put things in the proper sale to obtain the best price for them. In order to do this, you need accurate information about your pieces, plus knowing who might buy them, who might sell them advantageously, and what your expectations might be.

What gives a piece value? Is it "of the period"? This describes an 18th-century table made in 1749, not "in the style of" at a later date. The authenticity of a piece, proving it is not a reproduction or a forgery, is the controlling factor. The craftsmanship of a piece, for example, on an 18th-century Newport, Rhode Island, desk made by John Goddard or a 20th-century Tiffany glass lamp is valued. The artistic excellence of original Picasso or Rembrandt prints brings high prices.

The condition of a piece is a large factor in the marketability. If damaged, can it be restored? What would restoration cost you or the potential buyer? Is the piece in fashion? Objects can move in and out of fashion. Fashion for objects is like fashion in clothing. Are skirts up or down this year? When I was first married, I bought antique French paperweights from newspaper ads for under $200. Today, they go for thousands. There were few buyers at that time. Now antique paperweights are in fashion and there are many collectors. When they were first made, in the mid-1800s, in glass factories along with chandeliers, tableware, and toilet services, they were fashionable, but inexpensive.

Was the object made by a name designer, craftsman, or factory? A Dior creation, a Chippendale chair, or a Fabergé box garners grand prices. Was it ever in the possession of a famous person? A bonnet worn by Dolly Madison is highly desirable, while one owned by your ex-state senator may never be valuable. The sale of Charlie "Bird" Parker's saxophone for $144,000, double its estimate, and those of Greta Garbo's paintings and Merle Oberon's jewels, proves it pays to be famous. Size also plays a factor. A carpet may be exceptional, but if it is too large to fit in most rooms, it may not sell quickly. On the other hand, "great rooms" are now in fashion and your oversized carpet might bring an excellent price. What comes around goes around. Some sages say "keep things for three generations!"

Everyone wants to get the best price for their property. What is the best price? This is not easy to answer. I can quote recent high and low auction prices, note trends and discuss the economy but no one can predict a future sale. We can only estimate a probable figure from our knowledge of current prices, the look of the piece, its condition, rarity, appeal, and provenance. At auction, two similar pieces may be sold with the better one drawing a lower price. This may occur when a bidder fails to get the first piece, feels badly, and bids higher for the lesser one. The best price for most pieces may be a "satisfactory" price. This may not be the highest price ever realized, but not a low one either. A satisfactory price is realistic. The important thing is to choose the proper place to market your goods!

Every category of objects should be examined carefully. You will discover that the best place to sell particular things may vary. Even if you go to auction, you may need separate auctions or even different auction houses for various items.

Whatever you are planning to sell, you need to ask questions and receive answers. Check this book for specific information dealing with auctions, furniture, jewelry, appraisers, etc. Always get more than one professional opinion! Do not rely on the advice of friends or relatives!

If you are considering an auction sale, contact more than one house. Usually the larger auction houses have better catalogues, more advertising, and larger sales, which work in your favor. I live in the Chicago area, and would contact Leslie Hindman Auctioneer, John Hanzel Galleries or Dunning's in Elgin. In the sections on auctions, auction houses are listed by area. You might begin by contacting those in your area.

If an estate is to be settled, ask your estate lawyer for recommendations. Keep in mind that the lawyer usually wants to settle things quickly, which can be sensible, *but* may not bring you the greatest return.

Do you own special things, such as pedigree signed jewelry, rare books or antiques? Check magazines such as *Arts at Auction* for houses that specialize in the sale of these pieces. You might call or write to them for information concerning upcoming sales (see chapter on auctions for important, detailed information). These magazines also run dealer advertisements. Check these for a possible sale opportunity. Call them. Dealers always need merchandise.

It's easy to become confused. There are so many objects to keep track of, auction terms, dealer terms, and the unfamiliar vocabulary of selling. Learn what the words mean. Many are explained in this book. Don't be embarrassed to ask questions.

It's O.K. to admit you don't understand what someone is telling you. Many knowledgeable people are so familiar with their subject that they assume everyone else knows what they are talking about. It is intelligent to say, "I really don't follow what you just said. Would you please go over it again?" If you don't understand, it is possible you are hearing "double-talk." You have heard the saying "buyer beware." Sellers must also beware.

If you have a hearing or seeing problem, be up-front about it. I have thought people could hear me and later found they did not. Professionals often deal with people with these conditions and are understanding.

Whatever arrangements you make, get everything in writing. I can't repeat this often enough. Keep written records of each piece and where it is going. Put all contracts in a safe deposit box, but keep a copy at home for your daily use.

An article by Bob Jackman in *The Maine Digest* (December 1994) relates that last summer a two-and-a-half story home sold for $55,000. Among items auctioned off from this house were a stack of approximately 2,000 old comic books. They sold for $79,000. This does make you think. In the same issue these other items appear:

A 20-year collection of 26 barber poles were sold for $18,000;

A pair of scarecrows bought cheaply at a farm sale brought their owners $700;

A pair of hand-carved bookends fetched $170;

A circa 1800 18-hole candle mold of pewter sold for $1,650;

A circa 1850 kitchen worktable brought $495;

A French armoire with a mirrored door $3,600;

A pie safe with original paint was worth $1,650;

A cutesy primitive painting of a kitten brought $800;

A 19th-century harp sold for $3,850 although it needed restoration;

A ship in a bottle was purchased for $125.

Obviously many things you may possess are worth selling. It isn't only your silver punch bowl or antique dresser that can make you wealthier. Even simple kitchen utensils are worth from 25¢ up to many dollars. The combined value of many things that are found in homes all over the country can produce a large sum of money when sold.

WHAT TO DO, WHAT NOT TO DO

1. List the item or items to be sold. This is your inventory.

2. Do you know their current value? If so, record them and where your information came from. Do you have an updated appraisal? Is the appraisal for replacement or disposal? A replacement appraisal will probably list prices that you cannot realistically expect to achieve when selling.

3. If you do not know their value, consider calling an appraiser. Be certain that this appraiser is familiar with pieces such as yours. This is important! I speak from experience gained from dealing with appraisals that are plain wrong. A specialist in art glass may not know diddly about oriental carpets.

4. Consider contacting various auction houses. (See chapter on auctions.)

5. Check shops selling similar items. Go to antique shows to see if they are selling similar pieces. Speak with the dealers. Might they buy your pieces? Can they recommend other dealers?

6. Check price guides, such as *Kovels* or *Lyles*, for current prices.

7. If you are interested in a house sale, contact more than one agent. (See chapter on house sales.)

8. Should you contact a resale shop? Maybe. (See chapter on resale shops.)

9. Would you be willing to place an ad in a newspaper? Would you feel safe doing this?

10. Should you repair items or leave them alone? Get estimates? Use only experts for antique pieces. Check with auction houses, dealers or appraisers first.

11. Should you consider a donation and obtain a tax write-off? (See chapter on donations.)

12. Keep a list of appropriate names, addresses, phone numbers and prices in a folder or notebook.

13. Take close-up photographs and save the negatives. Date them. Put a set in your safe deposit box. If you are moving, these photographs will show the condition of the pieces in case of an accident while moving.

14. Whatever you decide, get the terms in writing. *Read* the terms before signing.

15. If you use an appraiser, have more than one copy of the appraisal made. Use one to work from and keep one in a vault.

16. If someone offers to help you sort things, do not give them objects in return. You might have a friend or domestic service person with very good taste who might walk off with a valuable piece. You can send a box of candy or offer lunch in appreciation.

17. An appraiser should never accept a piece as a gesture of friendship, or to buy or sell for you. This is not professional!

18. Begin to think like a dealer, not like a buyer.

We all prefer to deal with pleasant people, but charming people can sell us down the river. Many times clients have told me, "But he was such a nice man." I'm not recommending crabby people, but don't make decisions based on well-packaged charm and flattery.

Make decisions and handle your affairs responsibly. But don't rush because you are under stress. Remember, you don't have to do everything right this minute. There is usually a margin of time to reflect. You don't want to repent in leisure.

People often think if something is ugly, it is worthless. Not true. Conversely, because you think something is beautiful, that does not mean you will receive a great deal of money for it. "Reality must be considered" is a statement of fact. As an appraiser, I deal with people who are often unaware of the true worth of their possessions or have been misled. I find it difficult to inform someone that their family heirloom 18th-century French chair is, in reality, an early 20th-century English reproduction. On the other hand, I delight in informing a client those "ugly" watercolors that her deceased husband bought during a former marriage will bring six figures.

Do not take the advice of well-meaning friends unless they are actually experts. A professional appraiser, dealer or auction house will offer you infinitely better advice. What something sold for in 1970 or 1980 does not apply in the 1990s. You need to understand the current market. Most people really don't know what today's market can bring them. Recently an iron dog brought $7,500, an 1820 quilt made in New England sold for $12,000, a painted fire-board for $95,000, a pair of Chinese porcelain geese for $40,000, a 1925 hooked rug for $35,000, an American primitive portrait for $100,000, a Windsor armchair for $18,000, and a teddy bear for $86,350. These prices make doing your homework interesting.

Before you commit yourself to any sale, stop and consider keeping particular sentimental objects. You might regret parting with certain pieces. Many people regret the sale of various objects the rest of their lives. Widows moving to smaller quarters often make this mistake. Better to live in a home crowded with happy memories than a sparse magazine look-a-like room.

If you and your property are located in different places, especially different states, selling becomes more of a problem. Still, don't be rushed more than absolutely necessary. This often occurs while settling an estate or during a divorce. At least call an appraiser, if only for suggestions, before your final decisions. You may choose to store various pieces temporarily. Sometimes it helps to have pieces photographed and appraised before storing them. Each carton should be carefully marked so you can put them in a future sale without massive searching.

I know of a small estate consisting primarily of residential contents that was almost disposed of with a quick, no reserve, house sale. For whatever reason, the owner decided to call an auction house before she made up her mind. To shorten a long story, two tiny tea cups sold for $2,500. The house sale folk simply did not recognize the rarity of these cups. Many people worry about being taken advantage of. In truth, most mistakes are due to a lack of knowledge. The cups might have been sold for five dollars instead of $2,500, and no one would have been the wiser. Perhaps not even the buyer.

If you are dealing with many different types of residential contents—from a 10-year-old fridge to antique English furniture and maybe an oriental carpet, a painting, some art prints, and perhaps a glass collection—it becomes obvious that each piece might be sold at a different place or at a different auction. You have various options. The easiest way will probably not be the best way to realize the highest prices. Unfortunately, when you need to sell, chances are you will not fare as well as when you do not need to sell.

You can easily rent space at flea markets, antique shows and retail markets. If the law requires, apply to your state revenue department for a sales tax number. This is yet another popular way to sell possessions.

If you are interested in a house sale or a sale to a retail dealer, contact more than one. Each time you speak with an expert you may pick up helpful information. Write it down. Ask about potential prices and recently achieved prices for similar goods. It is important that you fully understand what you are doing. For instance, if you consign a piece to a resale shop, how much commission will you pay? Will that commission change if the piece does not sell in six weeks? Will the shop own it entirely if it does not sell in six months? If you use an auction house, what commission will they charge? If you leave it with a dealer, will they buy it outright or take it on consignment? Get all transactions in writing. Read the small print and ask questions, or you may simply be giving your things away. Check other chapters in this book for information on specific types of sales.

DEALING WITH INHERITANCE

If you have turned to this chapter, you probably want advice concerning estate liquidation and the disposal of certain pieces.

Start with your primary decisions. If you have inherited a house, do you want to put it on the market? Do you want to keep it for your own use or for rental? Have you discussed selling with your accountant and lawyer? If you plan to sell, have you contacted an agent? Certainly speak to more than one agent doing business in the area. Ask how many homes they have sold in this area and for what price. Can you negotiate the commission? Don't sign a contract unless you understand absolutely every aspect. Talk to your lawyer before signing any document. Might you consider selling the property yourself, thus saving the commission? What is involved? Only after making this important decision can you deal with the interior contents.

Now the real physical work begins. Everything must be sorted. Buy a notebook. Make a record of the pieces by category, such as furniture, glass, art, etc. Take photographs and keep the negatives in your vault. At this point consider hiring a residential contents appraiser. I would suggest this before you decide how you will sell the things you do not intend to keep. An appraiser may point out valuable pieces you are not aware of. Often people who bought things in their lifetime for everyday use were unaware of their subsequent importance. For example, an elderly couple who were moving called me to appraise their things. They knew their silver and various pieces of furniture were valuable but had no idea of a lamp worth thousands. It was a very important Arts and Crafts piece. The other side of the coin is that many pieces purchased by our ancestors were acquired at the peak of their popularity but have never achieved those highs since. So "don't count your chickens" until the checks are in the bank.

Don't assume everyday things are worthless. How about books—do you own first editions? One old record may not bring much, but how many are in the house? Everything adds up!

If you own things jointly, sit down and talk. Everyone has needs, opinions, potential problems and feelings. This, as you know, can be an unsettling time and old animosities may surface. Stay cool. If helpful, choose a role model and attempt to act as that person might under similar circumstances. If you don't know any good role models, consider "in the style of" Mother Theresa, Inspector Morse, Judge Ito, Barbara Walters or Ted Koppel.

1. Contact and set up appointments with your lawyer and accountant.

2. Find out if there is a will and what it provides.

3. If the estate is in excess of $600,000, expect to pay a federal estate tax.

4. Determine if you need to open a probate estate to transfer the property to the heirs or the devisees so that the heirs become the actual owners of the property.

5. Make an inventory of all property.

6. A security system must be set in place.

7. The value of property must be established. The use of a real estate appraiser or a residential contents appraiser is usually needed at this time.

8. Usually an estate appraiser uses a low auction figure to value estate property. However, if the estate is not

taxable, a higher valuation may be advantageous. The higher valuation will result in a higher basis in the asset and a smaller taxable gain in case of resale. The appraiser, however, must always be realistic and in the market range.

9. Are there existing insurance policies on items you have inherited? Check them carefully.

10. If more than one person has inherited, decisions as to division must be discussed.

11. If you are the only heir, you can please yourself.

12. Decide what, if any, pieces have sentimental value. Do you want to save particular pieces for children or grandchildren, nieces or nephews?

13. Whatever you decide, remember that everything in life is lent to us. Take good care of all your new possessions. Wrap breakables in bubble wrap. Chips, dents and nicks will affect their value. Use gentle hands so that you and another generation will enjoy these objects.

14. Everything is worth money. To sell carelessly is not smart. However, giving generously to family and friends produces a lasting ripple of affection. I treasure a small "made in Japan" pitcher my aunt Evelyn gave me over 30 years ago. Everything cannot be valued in terms of money.

It is a good idea to learn about the things you have inherited. What do you know about them? Are they historic? What was their country of origin? What period were they made in? Once you can identify them, it is possible to get a "ballpark" price. Learn how to use price guides and auction sheets. In England the value of a silver teapot or tray is lowered

50 percent if the original family crest is removed. In America, it rarely affects the value, but flatware sells better without monograms. How do you find the prices for '50s furniture? Chairs such as the Arne Jacobson egg or womb chair are more desirable with original upholstery. Furniture does not have to be 100 years old to have value. With all objects, the key is "of the period." This means original to the period. I have seen Eames plywood chairs at house sales for $10 that hammer down $300 at auction and more if three or more are offered. Are some of your books important? Should you contact a book seller early on or wait until the house is almost empty? What about quilts, tablecloths, and clothing? Are there any original garments by name designers? Jewelry might be an important part of your estate. When we really begin to separate the various things in any home, it becomes evident that even an average home has many, many objects of varying worth. Your job will be to sell those objects intelligently and make a healthy profit.

If objects are damaged, should you consider restoration? Certainly consult with a dealer or auction house before doing any tinkering. Less is more in most cases.

Now comes the decision of where to sell. Read the chapters on auction houses, house sales, dealer sales, classified sales and owner sales.

AUCTIONS

If I had to choose only one way to sell, I would choose going to auction. However, other ways to sell may also prove as successful. Dealer sales, house sales, mail sales, etc., are discussed in other chapters. This chapter is devoted to the auction market. An auction is a public sale where property goes to the highest bidder.

How does a seller choose an auction house? Notice, I use the word seller. If a buyer asked what auction or auction house, I might recommend a different one. A seller wants his or her property sold at an auction that will have many "like" things in it, ensuring many interested buyers. If you hope to sell a violin, it should not be lumped in with furniture, porcelain or books. If you want to buy a violin, however, this diverse sale might provide you with a fine violin bought cheaply, since musicians would probably not attend that sale.

While today there is a global auction market, particular pieces sell better in different parts of the country. For example, you would probably not sell southwestern art at an eastern sale for the same price that it would garner in the western states. Chicago silver, such as Kalo, will sell best in the Chicago area. Judgment must play a part in your decisions.

How does an auction house make money if it does not own any property? It is an agent and charges both the buyer and the seller a commission for their participation in the sale. This charge is not always the same. Different houses may have differing terms which often depend on the amount of the sale or the item. Can commissions be negotiated? Yes! Always negotiate. You may even be offered a free catalogue photograph. Always ask.

What will an auction house do for you? Sell your things for a good price. They can also value your pieces, help decide on the reserve, advertise in newspapers and magazines, send out catalogues to customers that request them, insure the pieces and even help you choose the proper auction for them. A well-run auction house can do all these things for you. Sometimes they can't or don't. Sometimes the fault is partially the seller's. A seller must ask the proper questions and find out certain information. Often an auction house representative will come to the house if, after talking to you, he or she believes it will benefit both.

Will certain auction houses do more for the client? You must contact more than one auction house and find out. Never accept only one opinion unless you are experienced with auction selling. Even if you have dealt successfully with an auction house previously, you should still ask questions of another, depending on what you plan to sell. For example, if you have rare books you are planning to auction, you could contact an auction house near you, but also contact one such as the Swann Auction house in New York that specializes in rare books.

Auction houses can arrange transportation of your pieces. There is usually a charge for this service.

What departments do auction houses have? This depends on the house. The larger houses have separate departments for furniture, art, musical instruments, etc., each with their own experts. The various departments produce catalogues for their sales. You can call or write for particular catalogues and also for realized prices. There is a charge for this service, but it's well worth the cost.

What category of object might an auction house handle? Sotheby's in New York offers sellers an amazing variety of sales such as: aeronautica; African art; American folk art; American Indian art; American manuscripts, paintings, drawings, and sculpture; antique jewelry; applied arts; arms and armor; Art Nouveau; atlases; maps; autographs; banknotes; bonds; baseball cards; books; British paintings, drawings, watercolors and pottery; cars; ceramics; Chinese art; comic books; and other collectibles. Obviously the large houses auction many types of objects. On the other hand, a smaller one specializing in a particular category might do better for you.

You should visit an auction viewing room if you are a potential seller. Are pieces arranged for good viewing? Go to a sale at an auction house before giving them your property to sell. If you don't live too far away, going to a sale will show you how that house conducts a sale. You may be impressed or not. What do you think of the security? Are items handled carefully? Have items been damaged? Is the auctioneer impressive? Have they garnered a large crowd of bidders? Is the auction selling over estimates?

Auction houses conduct more than one type of auction. They usually have auctions that deal with specific items, listed in a catalogue with a reserve. A "reserve" is the minimum price for which an item will be sold. They may also have auctions where property is sold with no reserves. An unreserved auction means the article goes to the highest bidder no matter how low the last bid is. This is a "cash and carry" type of procedure.

What happens if someone wants to bid on an item but cannot attend the auction? This person leaves an absentee or pocket bid for the item, which can be mailed in or delivered in person before the sale. The record of absentee bids is kept by the house and is given the same recognition as bids made during a sale. The record of an absentee bid is termed "book." Telephone bids are accepted as well. Many items are sold successfully in this way.

When a piece is described "as is," it means the article is in some way damaged and will be sold in that condition. Auction houses are usually honest in this description. If they were known to be deceptive, buyers would go elsewhere.

Pieces are insured while at an auction house. However, you should discuss how much the piece or pieces will be insured for. Some houses use the low estimate. Check the terms on your consignment contract.

When you agree to offer certain merchandise to an auction house, you will be asked to sign a consignment agreement. You should read any contract with the auction house carefully before you sign it. Reading it may trigger questions that you should be asking before you sign. Listed in the contract will be the financial terms. It might state 25 percent at or below $500, 15 percent at or below $1,999, or 10 percent above $1,999, or five percent buy-in. There might be one percent for insurance, the cost for an illustration in the catalogue and a minimum commission per lot.

The contract will contain the date and receipt number, and the items you have agreed to offer will be listed along with the reserve, the sale date and the lot number.

On the reverse side of this consignment agreement will be conditions. They may include the right of the house to withdraw any property before the sale at its discretion. In addition, the commission will be explained. The packing and shipping charges will also be laid out and illustration charges will be noted.

Additional charges for services such as framing, restoration, independent appraisal, etc., will be explained. Insurance costs will be listed. Loss or damage to your property will be discussed, explaining the liability of the house.

You must describe your title to the property and that it is free of any claims. The contract may also contain estimates, catalogue descriptions, reserves, terms of withdrawal of property, how unsold property will be handled ("bought-in"), use or not of your name in the catalogue, the settlement check schedule, and governing laws concerning the agreement. You must be acquainted with all the terms of the agreement before you sign it.

What about after the auction sales? Many auction houses will take offers for unsold pieces after the actual auction. If they receive an offer for your property, they must call and get your permission to sell the piece, obviously for less than was originally asked. You will still pay the house their commission.

NORTH AMERICAN AUCTION HOUSES

New York City

Christie's
502 Park Ave.
New York, NY 10022
(212) 546-1000

Christie's East
219 E. 67th St.
New York, NY 10021
(212) 606-0400

Doyle
William Doyle Galleries
175 E. 87th St.
New York, NY 10128
(212) 427-2730

Great Gatsby's
91 University Place
New York, NY 10203
(800) 342-1744

Guernsey's
108 E. 73rd St.
New York, NY 10021

Harmer
Harmer Rooke
 Numismatists, Ltd.
3 E. 57th St.
New York, NY 10022
(212) 751-1900

Harmers
H. R. Harmer Inc.
14 E. 33rd St.
New York, NY 10036
(212) 532-3700
(800) 223-6076

Hôtel des Encans New York
129 E. 61st St., #3
New York, NY 10021
(212) 980-2003

Illustration House, Inc.
96 Spring St.
New York, NY 10012
(212) 966-9444

Ivy & Mader
Philatelic Auctions Inc.
32 E. 57th St.
New York, NY 10022
(212) 486-1222

Lubin Galleries
30 W. 26th St.
New York, NY 10001
(212) 924-3777

Metropolitan Arts and
   Antiques Pavilion
110 W. 19th St.
New York, NY 10011
(212) 463-0200

Morrell & Co.
Fine Wine Auctions
535 Madison Ave.
New York, NY 10022
(212) 688-9370

Phillips New York
406 E. 79th Street
New York, NY 10021
(212) 570-4830

Poster Auctions
   International, Inc.
37 Riverside Dr.
New York, NY 10023
(212) 787-4000

Robert A. Siegel
65 E. 55th St.
17th Floor
New York, NY 10022
(212) 753-6421

R.M. Smythe & Co.
26 Broadway
New York, NY 10004
(212) 908-4006

Sotheby's
1334 York Ave.
New York, NY 10021
(212) 606-7000

Stack's Coin Co.
123 W. 57th St.
New York, NY 10019
(212) 582-2580

Swann Galleries
104 E. 25th St.
New York, NY 10010
(212) 254-4710

Tepper Galleries
110 E. 25th St.
New York, NY 10010
(212) 677-5300

New England

F. O. Bailey & Co.
141 Middle St.
Portland, ME 04101
(207) 774-1479

James R. Bakker, Inc.
370 Broadway
Cambridge, MA 02139
(617) 864-7067

Barridoff Galleries
Box 9715
Portland, ME 04104
(207) 772-5011

Berman's Auction Gallery
33 W. Blackwell St.
Dover, NJ 07801
(201) 361-3110

Ronald Bourgeault
Northeast Auctions
694 Lafayette Rd.
Hampton, NH 03842
(603) 926-8222

Bowers & Merena Galleries
Box 1224
Wolfeboro, NH 03894
(603) 569-5095

Bradford Auction Gallery
Box 160, Route 7
Sheffield, MA 01257
(413) 229-6667

Caropreso Gallery
Jennifer House Commons
Stockbridge Rd., Route 7
Great Barrington, MA
(413) 528-8280

Castner's
Box 920, 6 Wantage Ave.
Route 519
Branchville, NJ 07826
(201) 948-3868

Bob & Sallie Connelly
666 Chenango St.
Binghampton, NY 13901
(607) 722-9593

Dargate Auction Galleries
6000 Penn Circle South
Pittsburgh, PA 15206
(412) 362-3558

Douglas Auctioneers
Route 5
South Deerfield, MA 01373
(413) 665-2877

Robert C. Eldred & Co.
Box 796, Route 6A
Dennis, MA 02641
(508) 385-3116

Robert Foster
Box 203
Newcastle, ME 04553
(207) 563-8150

Freeman/Fine Arts of
   Philadelphia, Inc.
1810 Chestnut St.
Philadelphia, PA 19103
(215) 563-9275

Grogan & Co.
890 Commonwealth Ave.
Boston, MA 02215
(617) 566-4100

C. E. Guarino
Box 49
Denmark, ME 04022
(207) 452-2123

Hesse Galleries
20 Main St.
Otego, NY 13825
(607) 988-6322

Greg Manning Auctions, Inc.
115 Main Rd.
Montville, NJ 07045
(201) 299-1800

Mapes Auctioneers
1729 Vestal Parkway, West
Vestal, NY 13850
(607) 754-9293

Maritime Antique Auctions
R R #2, Box 322
York, ME 03909
(207) 363-4247

Mystic Fine Arts
47 Holmes St.
Mystic, CT 06355
(203) 572-8873

New England Fine Art
    Auctions, Inc.
Box 15, Hopedale Business
    Park
Hopedale, MA 01747
(508) 473-9422

Rafael Osona
Box 2607
Nantucket, MA 02584
(508) 228-3942

David Rago
9 S. Main St.
Lambertville, NJ 08530
(609) 397-9374

Riba Auctions
Box 53
South Glastonbury, CT 06753
(203) 633-3076

Bob, Chuck & Rich Roan, Inc.
Box 118 RD 3
Cogan Station, PA 17728
(717) 494-0170

Sandwich Auction House
15 Tupper Rd.
Sandwich, MA 02563
(508) 888-1926

Savoia's
Route 23
South Cairo, NY 12482
(518) 622-8000

Skinner/Bolton
Skinner, Inc.
357 Main St., Route 117
Bolton, MA 01740
(508) 779-6241

Skinner/Boston
Skinner, Inc.,
The Heritage On The Garden
63 Park Plaza
Boston, MA 02116
(617) 350-5400
(617) 350-5429 fax

Stonington Fine Arts
143 Water St.
Stonington, CT
(203) 535-4956

H. R. Tyrer Galleries
170 Glen St.
Glens Falls, NY 12801
(518) 793-2244

Adam A. Weschler & Son
909 E. St., NW
Washington, DC 20004
(202) 628-1281

Willis Henry Auctions
22 Main St.
Marshfield, MA 02050
(617) 834-7774

Winter Associates Inc.
21 Cooke St.
Plainville, CT 06062
(203) 793-0288

Richard W. Withington
590 Center Rd.
Hillsboro, NH 03244
(603) 464-3232

Young Fine Arts Gallery, Inc.
Box 313, North
Berwick, ME 03906
(207) 676-3104

Samuel Yudkin & Associates
The Woodner, Room A232
3636 16th St., NW
Washington, DC 20010
(202) 232-6249

Midwest

Frank H. Boos Gallery
420 Enterprise Ct.
Bloomfield Hills, MI 48302
(313) 332-1500

Chicago Art Galleries, Inc.
5039 Oakton St.
Skokie, IL 60077
(708) 677-6080

Du Mouchelle Art Galleries
409 E. Jefferson Ave.
Detroit, MI 48226
(313) 963-6255

Dunning's Auction Service,
    Inc.
325 W. Huron
Chicago, IL 60610
(312) 664-8400

Early Auctions Co.
123 Main St.
Milford, OH 45150
(513) 831-4833

Charles G. Firby
6695 Highland Rd.
Suite 106
Waterford, MI 48327
(313) 666-3946

Garth/Garth Stratford
Garth's Auctions
2690/2730 Stratford Rd.,
    Box 369
Delaware, OH 43015
(614) 362-4771

Hanzel Galleries Inc.
1120 S. Michigan Ave.
Chicago, IL 60605
(312) 922-6234

Harris Antique
Gene Harris Antique Auction
    Center, Inc.
203 S. 18th Ave.
Marshalltown, IA 50158
(515) 752-0600

Leslie Hindman Auctioneers
215 W. Ohio St.
Chicago, IL 60610
(312) 670-0010

Joy Luke Fine Arts
300 E. Grove St.
Bloomington, IL 61701
(309) 828-5533

Main Auction Galleries Inc.
137 W. 4th St.
Cincinnati, OH 45202
(513) 621-1280

Old World Ltd.
7438 W. North Ave.
Elmwood Park, IL 60635
(708) 456-7730

Park West Gallery, Inc.
29469 Northwestern
    Highway
Southfield, MI 48034
(313) 354-2343
(800) 521-9654

Schrager Auction Galleries,
    Ltd.
2915 N. Sherman Blvd.,
    Box 10390
Milwaukee, WI 53210
(414) 873-9985/3738

Selkirk Galleries
4166 Olive St.
St. Louis, MO 63108
(314) 533-1700

Don Treadway
2128 Madison Rd.
Cincinnati, OH 45208
(513) 321-6742

Wolf's
1239 W. Sixth
Cleveland, OH 44113
(216) 575-9653

West

A.N. Abell Auction Company
2613 Yates Avenue
Commerce, CA 90040
(213) 734-4151

Allard Indian Auctions
Box 460
St. Ignatius, MT 59865
(406) 745-2951

Butterfield & Butterfield
220 San Bruno Ave., at
    15th St.
San Francisco, CA 94103
(415) 861-7500

Butterfield/LA
Butterfield & Butterfield
7601 Sunset Blvd.
Los Angeles, CA 90046
(213) 850-7500

Camden House Auctioneers,
    Inc.
427 N. Canon Dr.
Beverly Hills, CA 90210
(310) 246-1212

Christie's/BH
342 N. Rodeo Dr.
Beverly Hills, CA 90210
(213) 275-5534

Harvey Clar Auctioneers
    and Appraisers
5644 Telegraph Ave.
Oakland, CA 94609
(510) 428-0100

Colonial Stamp Co.
5757 Wilshire Blvd.
Penthouse 8
Los Angeles, CA 90036
(213) 933-9435

Fifth Avenue Gallery
60 Fifth Avenue
Redwood City, CA 94063
(415) 363-0443

File's Auctioneering &
    Fine Art
200 N. Main St.
Santa Ana, CA 92701
(714) 547-1415

Joel L. Malter & Co., Inc.
17005 Ventura Blvd.
Encino, CA 91436
(818) 784-7772

John Moran
3202 E. Foothill Blvd.
Pasadena, CA 91107
(818) 793-1833

Neale & Sons, Inc.
14320 S. Saratoga-Sunnyvale
    Rd.
Box 425
Saratoga, CA 95071-0425
(408) 867-3751

O'Gallerie, Inc.
228 N.E. 7th Ave.
Portland, OR 97232
(503) 238-0202

Satori Fine Art Auctioneers
2305 Fifth Ave.
Seattle, WA 98121
(206) 443-3666

Selman L.H.
Selman Ltd.
761 Chestnut St.
Santa Cruz, CA 95060
(408) 427-1177

Sotheby's Jewelry West
308 N. Rodeo Dr.
Beverly Hills, CA 90210
(213) 274-0340

Superior Stamp & Coin
An A-Mark Company
9478 W. Olympic Blvd.
Beverly Hills, CA 90212
(310) 203-9855

Southwest

Dan May & Associates
4110 N. Scottsdale Rd., #105
Scottsdale, AZ 85251
(602) 941-4200

Southeast

Charlton Hall Galleries, Inc.
929 Gervais St.
Columbia, SC 29201
(803) 779-5678

J. G. Cochran Auctioneers
    & Associates, Ltd.
7704 Mapleville Rd., Box 222
Boonsboro, MD 21713
(301) 739-0538
(301) 432-2844

Harris Auction Galleries
875 N. Howard St.
Baltimore, MD 21201
(410) 728-7040

James D. Julia
Route 201
Fairfield, ME 04937
(207) 453-7125

Lincoln Galleries
225 Scotland Rd.
Orange, NJ 07050
(201) 677-2000

Luper Auction Galleries, Inc.
Box 5143, 1515 W. Broad St.
Richmond, VA 23220
(804) 359-2493

Merrill's Auction Gallery
32 Beacon St., South
Burlington, VT 05401
(802) 878-2625

Northgate Gallery
5520 Highway 153
Chattanooga, TN 37343
(615) 877-6114

Alfred A. Robinson
   Company
509 Cooper St., Box 3038
Knoxville, TN 37917
(615) 522-9708

C. G. Sloan & Co.
4950 Wyaconda Rd.
North Bethesda, MD 20852
(301) 468-4911

Kimball M. Sterling, Inc.
   Auctions
125 W. Market St.
Johnson City, TN 37601
(615) 928-1471

Theriault's
Box 151
Annapolis, MD 21404
(410) 224-3655

South

C.B. Charles Galleries, Inc.
750 E. Sample Rd., Suite 6
Pompano Beach, FL 33064
(305) 946-1800

Jim Depew Galleries, Inc.
1860 Piedmont Rd., N.E.
Atlanta, GA 30324
(404) 874-2286

Garrett Galleries, Inc.
1800 Irving Blvd.
Dallas, TX 75207
(214) 742-4343

Goldberg Auction Galleries,
   Inc.
547 Baronne St.
New Orleans, LA 70176
(504) 592-2300

Great Gatsby's
5070 Peachtree Industrial Blvd.
Atlanta, GA 30341
(404) 457-1905

Hart Galleries
2301 S. Voss Rd.
Houston, TX 77057
(713) 266-3500

Heritage Numismatic
  Auctions, Inc.
100 Heritage Plaza
Highland Park Village
Dallas, TX 75205
(214) 528-3500
(800) US-COINS

Ivy, Shreve & Mader Philatelic
  Auctions, Inc.
100 Heritage Plaza
Highland Park Village
Dallas, TX 75205
(214) 528-3500
(800) 782-6771

Myers Auction Gallery
1600 4th St., North
St. Petersburg, FL 33704
(813) 823-3249

Neal Auction Co.
4038 Magazine St.
New Orleans, LA 70115
(504) 899-5329

New Orleans Auction
  Galleries, Inc.
801 Magazine St.
New Orleans, LA 70130
(504) 566-1849

Red Baron's Antiques
6450 Roswell Rd.
Atlanta, GA 30328
(404) 252-3770

Canada

Christie's/T
170 Bloor St., Suite 210
Toronto, ON
Canada M5S 1T9
(416) 960-2063

Robert Deveau Galleries
297-299 Queen St., East
Toronto, ON
Canada M5A 1S7
(416) 364-6271

F. E. Eaton & Sons
One Bentall Centre
505 Burrard St., Suite 1860
Vancouver, B.C.
Canada V7X 1M6
(604) 689-3118

Empire/M
Empire Industries
5500 Paré St.
Montreal, PQ
Canada H4P 2M1
(514) 737-6586

Empire/O
1380 Cyrville Rd.
Gloucester, ON
Canada K1B 3L9
(613) 748-5342

Empire/T
165 Tycos Drive
North York, ON
Canada M6B 1W6
(416) 784-4261

Fraser-Pinneys Auctions
8290 Devonshire
Montreal, PQ
Canada H4P 2P7
(514) 345-0571

Gallery 68 Auctions
3 Southvale Dr.
Toronto, ON
Canada M4G 1G1
(416) 421-7614

Gardner's Auction Galleries
186 York Street
London, ON
Canada N6A 1B5
(519) 439-333

Hopmeyer & Jennings
Auctioneers & Appraisers
145 Davenport Rd.
Toronto, ON
Canada M5R 1J1
(416) 323-3166

Hotel des Encans
2825 Bates St.
Montreal, PQ
Canada H3S 1B3
(514) 344-4081

Joyner Fine Art Inc.
222 Gerrard St. East
Toronto, ON
Canada M5A 2E8
(416) 323-0909

Phillips Ward-Price
5A Thorncliffe Ave.
Toronto, ON
Canada M4K 1V4
(416) 462-9004

D&J Ritchie
288 King St. East
Toronto, ON
Canada M5A 1K4
(416) 364-1864

Sotheby's/T
9 Hazelton Ave.
Toronto, ON
Canada M5R 2E1
(416) 926-1774

Waddington, McLean & Co.
189 Queen St., East
Toronto, ON
Canada M5A 1S2
(416) 362-1678

International

Galerias Louis C. Morton
Monte Athos 179
Col. Lomas Virreyes, C.P.
D.F. 11000
Mexico
(05) 520-5005

SELLING OVER THE INTERNET

The Internet is a new tool for sellers. I stress the word "new." Thus far, buying and selling in cyberspace has lacked a technical mechanism for making purchases electronically interesting. Internet "addresses" may change often, so you must keep up and check for this.

In order to find out what is available on the Internet, a web browser from on-line services such as Prodigy, Compu-Serve, America Online, Mosaic or Microsoft Explorer is necessary. Netscape can browse and also publish.

A new company called Onsale, of Mountain View, California, is now in business. This Internet on-line auction service offers rare and collectible goods including fine wines, autographed sports jerseys, vintage computer equipment, and rock memorabilia. Visitors to Onsale's auction house (http://www.onsale.com) can submit merchandise and bids at this address. Bidders are required to submit a valid credit card number and an electronic mail (e-mail) address to Onsale over the Internet. There is an additional shipping and handling charge. Onsale, of course, takes a commission.

A World Wide Web home page displays the object to be sold, the minimum bid, bid increments, minimum price, quantity available, auction closing, seller, and a description of the article.

The World Wide Web, or WWW, or The Web to its friends, is a tool for navigating the Internet. It handles graphics and sounds as well as text. By clicking on icons, buyers can find sellers' home pages used to show merchandise.

Another way to sell is with Use Net. Use Net is to the Internet what the classifieds are to local newspapers. Sellers place their information on the Internet through Use Net, which will advertise the items they wish to sell. Like other mail sales, the buyer may return the item for various reasons. It pays to give careful information.

Here is a list of various selling opportunities available on the Internet:

Christie's—http://www.christies.com.

Index—Internet Resource Listing for Auctions. Here you'll find a directory of auction house home pages from all over the Net: cars, art, antiques, and government auctions: http://www.syspac.com/usaweb/auction.html.

Antiques & Collectibles On-Line—Information for collectors and dealers of all types of antiques and collectibles: http://www.antiques-on-line.com.

Antique Networking, Inc.—An on-line database designed to network buyers and sellers of high-end antiques locally, nationally, and internationally. It is utilized by antique dealers and their customers, brokers, collectors, trade show organizers, and repair/restoration shops: http://www.smart-pages.com/antique/index.html.

Recommended reading for Internet selling: *Vulcans Computer Monthly, Computer's Shopper—Sellers & Board-Watch Magazine, Advertising Age*, the book *Internet For Dummies*, by John Levine and Carol Baroudi (IDG Books, San Mateo, California).

Many local computer newspapers publish lists of "bulletin boards" where you can place ads.

You might subscribe to *Internet World*, P.O. Box 173, Mount Morris, IL, 61054 (800-573-3062) as another outlet.

CHARITABLE PROPERTY
CONTRIBUTIONS

Museums appreciate the generosity of their members and friends. The government wishes to encourage charitable contributions and, therefore, allows tax deductions. If you have reached a point in your life such as a move, an inheritance, or have a desire to enrich the museum, this might be a good time to donate art. Art works do not have to be circa anything but must have artistic value and be original.

The IRS has a rather complicated set of regulations dealing with such contributions. They are designed to protect you, the museum and the government. Always consult your lawyer and accountant.

Generally the amount of a charitable deduction for a contribution of property (other than money) is the fair market value of the piece. It is reported on Schedule A of Federal Income Tax Form 1040 under "Gifts to Charity."

If the deduction claimed exceeds $500, Form 8283, "Non-Cash Charitable Contributions," must be completed. If the claim is between $500 and $5,000, additional information is required: date of contribution, date and manner of acquisition by donor (you), adjusted basis and method used to determine the fair market value.

Any item which exceeds $5,000 must be reported in Section B of Federal Income Tax Form 8283. For these more valuable donations, you must satisfy additional requirements. These include a "qualified appraisal" which must be summarized and attached to your return.

The "qualified appraisal" is one made not more than 60 days before the date of the contribution. It must give a detailed description of the property and the date of the contribution. It should also state the terms of any agreement relating to the use, sale or disposition of the donated property. The qualified appraiser should be identified by name, taxpayer identification number, and list the appraiser's qualifications including background, experience, education and professional affiliations.

The appraisal must state that it was prepared for income tax purposes, the date on which the property was valued, the fair market value on the date of contribution and the method of appraisal used. Obviously, you can't use an old insurance appraisal.

Be aware that limits exist on the total amount of charitable contributions allowed as deductions.

Many charitable organizations appreciate donations of books, clothing, furniture, etc. In return they should provide you with a donation form that you can attach to your tax form, detailing your gift and its worth. Do not donate any property unless such a form will be issued to you.

If you donate books, keep a list by title, author, condition, and edition. Obviously a first edition of most books will be worth more than a later edition. I do not advise merely putting a 50¢ value on each book.

The same advice goes with any donation of clothes. If you are donating designer clothes, put down the name of the designer and year it was sold. Of course you cannot take the original cost as a deduction, but these garments are worth more than any old suit since they will bring more in a resale.

Everything takes time. It's best if you simply get on with it rather than think about doing the job. The doing can go quickly if you apply yourself to the task. As with all methods of disposal, you must sort items into categories.

Do not overlook contributions of historical value. These can range from vintage clothes to old report cards, union cards, draft information, photographs, catalogues, and so on. If you possess articles you think might interest your local historical society, call them. It's a great feeling to contribute to history.

The write-off possible is secondary to your participation in history. Museums and historical societies will record your gift with your name as the donor and the name of the original owner. If shown in an exhibition, you will be listed. Not only you, but your entire family will enjoy this honor. The Chicago Historical Society recently had an exhibition on Jewish immigrant women and used many donated clothes and personal items, as well as old photographs. Items displayed listed the donors' names and identified the people in the photographs. These donations required no money, but no amount of money could have given the donors more pleasure and pride.

SALES WITHIN COMPANIES

Many companies and firms have in-house sales. Employees of the company may advertise the sale of particular items every week. Let's take one such company newsletter called "Anything Goes." If an employee wants to advertise he may notify Miss X by 3:00 on Wednesday. This company also conducts a holiday bazaar at Christmas. Booths can be reserved for those with a lot to sell.

Listed in the "Anything Goes" newsletter are the items for sale and where to reach the seller. Many items are offered, such as evening purses, sport cards, printers, watches, furniture, pets, sale certificates, hand-crafted gifts, jewelry and cosmetics. Some items are printed in the newsletter and some are not.

If you work for a company that offers this type of sale, consider selling some of your possessions in this way.

If you don't, you might want to start such a sales program for your company. It is a great idea and does not carry the risk that a newspaper ad with strangers coming to your home may entail.

SELLING BY MAIL

Before you compose an ad to sell anything, you need to write an accurate description of the item. If you are familiar with auction catalogues, this will not be difficult. If you are not, the task will take more effort. What is a description? If you hope to sell a table by mail, you might write: "Table for sale. American Colonial Revival Butterfly Maple Table. Top Replaced. Late 19th Century. Height 25", width 13", depth 22". Price $600. Picture on request." In listing your items, be sure you include your name, box number or address, including city, state, and zip code. I do not advise offering damaged goods for a mail sale. You must be prepared to accept merchandise back if the customer is not satisfied. You would then lose the cost of shipping and packing.

You must decide where to place your ad and find out what the ad will cost. Perhaps you should check out various trading newspapers. What about local newspapers? Have you checked ads in magazines? If you hope to sell collectibles, the *Antique Trader* might do best for you. The magazine *Antique Toy World* is geared to the sale of toys. Check with your local library. They are a great source of information, and have many periodicals in their reading rooms.

When you receive a check, do not send the article until the check clears. Be especially careful of any check without a printed name. Keep a file on all sales and correspondence.

When mailing the purchased item, be sure it is insured. Send a copy of the bill with the item for sale, always keeping the original for yourself. If paid, mark the invoice "paid in full." It is also nice to include a thank you and sign your name.

If the post office has delivered your package damaged, the buyer must keep the damaged property. They must take it to the post office to process a claim. All the wrappings should be kept.

HOUSE SALES

A house sale is one way to completely clear out a house or apartment. This type of sale is often used to sell inherited property, to divide marital residential assets in a divorce or when persons plan to relocate, leaving many of their household pieces behind. For the persons or family who want to sell everything at one time, this type of sale might be the answer.

A house sale can provide the seller with various special services. A house sale service, as spelled out in the contract, can provide a cleaning service, write up the inventory, price the sale items, handle the advertising, present the pieces to their advantage, handle the actual sale and, ultimately, the payment check.

House sale services are listed in local phone books and can be found in the classified section of the newspaper. Your estate, divorce or family lawyer may also be able to recommend one or two services with good reputations.

Each contract will indicate the dates of the sale, services and sales commission. In this type of sale, as with all types, a contract must be agreed upon and signed. Often there is a sliding commission clause. Read the contract very carefully before you sign. Do not suppose! Ask questions and fully understand the answers. "What ifs" should be addressed before you sign a contract.

A well-run house sale gives out numbers to people when they arrive. First come, first serve is the rule. The sales people will allow only a designated number of people in at one time. This is a proper security measure. Plain clothes security may be used if considered necessary. Customers can leave a written bid on pieces at the price they are willing to pay. The sales people will call them if the property does not sell at the set price.

A house sale will sell everything on the premises. People are amazed how even small prices—such as kitchen utensils bring—add up. Items that might otherwise be tossed are someone's treasures. People go to sales searching for every conceivable type of item from matchbooks, toys, hats, ashtrays, photographs, old road maps, postcards to dining room sets and chandeliers. Major items include furniture, window treatments, rugs, jewelry, linens, crystal, silver, power tools, pictures and even automobiles.

House sale people may also conduct a family auction on the premises. This is a family-only sale for joint heirs and is an informal procedure. Many auction houses also offer this service.

House sales can be combined with auction sales. If you are selling a fine violin, a collection of Georgian silver, fine art or sculpture, rare books or art glass, etc., these particular pieces should be placed in separate auction sales. Pieces such as these are the reason dealers and pickers haunt house sales. It pays to separate the valuable from the ordinary and sell these pieces at auction.

When choosing a house sale service, consider the reputation of the sale people (get recent references), the security offered, insurance on your property, use of an appraiser, if needed, and the amount and type of advertising that will be used. House sale services should send out notices to regular patrons providing dates, locations, and contents of coming sales, as well as advertising in local newspapers.

Consider the people themselves. If you don't reside in the property that houses the potential sale, you may not have to spend a great deal of time with them. However, if you live on the site, you should engage persons that are compatible. They will be working in your home for days as it is time-consuming to inventory, price, display, and arrange a sale. If you are allergic to smoke or perfume, do not hire chain-smokers, or gardenia-musk-wearers. Personalities count in close encounters. Pat Drew of McDrew Sales (Kenilworth, IL) impressed me when she said she hopes to leave each sale with a new friend. Sellers must also cooperate, be helpful and keep children and animals from distracting the sales team.

Some recent house sale prices achieved are $8,000 for a 19th-century tapestry, twelve place settings of Herend china for $2,500, a Steuben vase for $250, a maple bedroom set for $500, twelve place settings of Kirk sterling for $2,100, a linen tablecloth with cut work and twelve napkins for $650, a Regency bookcase for $3,200, an egg beater for 25¢, a garden hose for $3.50 and a lamp for $35.

GARAGE SALES

This is a wonderful type of sale. You will pay no taxes as the items will sell for less than you originally paid for them. This is a grand way to turn unneeded things into cash. However, you will need the skill of a general and the cooperation of a sergeant and a few privates.

First begin an inventory. Leave room after the listed items for the price. Check your basement, garage, attic, closets and drawers for stock. List the items by category, if possible. Kitchen articles, garden equipment, tools, clothing, toys, books, children's clothes, nursery furniture, costume jewelry, suitcases, closet hangers, bolts of fabric, curtains, furniture, etc. Even cars can be sold in a garage sale.

Next, decide if you want to include items that belong to other family members, friends or neighbors. It might ensure additional workers. You will need help. Hopefully, you have someone with a strong back who can assist in the setting up of the sale. This is very hard work.

Once you have decided to have a garage sale, you need to pick a date. Then you can do some advertising. Many cities and villages offer garage sale signs that can be put up at your corner or in front of your home on the sale days. You might also put up a notice in your market and wherever notices are allowed. An ad in your local paper would be very helpful.

A space has to be cleared and set up a few days prior to the sale. Usually this is in the garage. The day of the sale, items will probably be displayed in the driveway or yard, as well as in the garage. Use your additional helpers to keep an eye on things and to answer questions.

Some items can be very useful, such as a clothes rack for clothing, one or more long tables to display your wares, a card table where a list of items and their prices and a money box can be situated, and two chairs. The list and box must never be left unattended.

It takes time to price items so begin that task early. You might go to other garage sales for ideas and pricing guidance. You may be surprised to see people rummaging in boxes searching for old matchbooks, coasters, ashtrays, baby shoes, playing cards, sports memorabilia, bits of lace, tiny china dolls, and metal candy boxes. Put out everything. Your junk is someone's treasure. I found a great ashtray at my neighbor's garage sale for one dollar. It is a signed French porcelain piece and advertises a famous club. I love it! Garage sales are irresistible to many people. They are a treasure just waiting to be discovered.

You will need some cash on hand. Go to the bank the day before and pick up 50 single dollars and a few dollars in change. I would suggest keeping most of the money in the house until actually needed. Be cautious of checks. Do not take any check without a name and address printed on it. Offer to hold an item so the buyer can cash a check at a bank or market nearby. Cash is best!

If you run into a bad weather day, reschedule the sale for another day. If you are seen doing a brisk business, neighbors might ask if they can bring some of their things over. Sure, why not? The larger your sale, the more people will stop, and this will give your items more public exposure.

Finally, consider the social aspect. Your neighbors will come to browse and visit and enjoy the event. When the sale is over, you will be wealthier and up on neighborhood news. You might decide to have a biyearly sale. Start saving.

PAWNBROKERS

A pawnbroker is a person whose shop lends money on articles of clothing, such as furs, watches, jewelry, televisions, computers and so on. These articles are left as security with the pawnbroker, who has the right to sell them if the loan is not repaid with interest and charges due within a certain time. People will always need money in a hurry. The moneylender can give you money quickly; however, the high interest rate is a down side.

What is a pawnshop? You see them in and around cities and you may have been wondering how they work. Pawnshops date back to ancient times and are one of the earliest recorded lending institutions. During the late Middle Ages the House of Lombard in Europe had a group of pawnshops. The sign of the House of Lombard was the three golden balls, and this sign was associated for years with the pawn industry. The pawn industry came to America with the first settlers, and in the early part of this century pawnbroking was regarded as the main source of consumer credit. With the rise of large consumer credit institutions, such as finance corporations, savings and loan associations, and credit unions, the pawnshop still plays a vital role in providing consumer credit. Sometimes the general public needs to borrow small sums of money that other sources are not willing to provide, and this has contributed to the rise in popularity of pawnshops. What chance do you have of securing a small loan of $100-$1000 from a financial institution for a two-week period? The cost of paperwork alone prohibits them from making such loans on a regular basis.

Pawnshop customers usually do not regard the transaction as a sale of their goods. They expect to pay back the loan and redeem their property. Pawnbrokers make it possible for a person without employment or in financial distress to obtain credit quickly, even in an unfamiliar city.

In most states, laws restrict the maximum interest rates a pawnbroker may charge. Regulations require the pawnbroker to keep a record book which contains a description of every article received.

Let's say you bring a piece of jewelry to a pawnbroker. If you and the pawnbroker reach an agreement on the amount of the loan, the pawnbroker will issue you, the customer, a pawn ticket which is a contract that states the amount of the loan, the pawn service charge, and the specified time that the pawnbroker will hold your personal property. The pawnbroker must live up to everything in the contract. He has to hold the property for the specified time and must take care of the property. You, the customer, know exactly what to expect. There should be no hidden charges. If you cannot redeem your property at the proper time, new arrangements may be made. If not, the broker is entitled to sell your property.

All types of people may occasionally need a pawnbroker. In certain scenarios such as before an estate is settled, it may become necessary to have some money quickly. This is one possibility. Be sure you understand the interest rates. Obviously, you must actually own any article you pawn.

The accepting of stolen property by a pawnshop is rare. When it does happen, the pawnbroker works with local law enforcement officials to see that justice is carried out. The pawn industry is a very closely regulated business. It is regulated by state, county, and local governments. A pawnbroker is required to turn in copies of the transactions where he acquires merchandise to local law enforcement officials. Also, a pawnbroker is required to maintain minimum assets to conduct his business. A pawnbroker also has a considerable investment in his business that he would be risking by knowingly taking in stolen property. The pawnbroker can be—and often is—one of the policeman's greatest friends in helping to curtail crime.

SELLING A CAR

How do you find out what a used car is worth? You might visit used-car lots. If you travel to enough of them, you may find a similar car and can check out the price. Checking the classifieds will allow you to see what other sellers are asking. Prices are usually inflated to allow room to negotiate. You can also call your local bank or savings and loan and ask an official to look up the car model in used car value guides such as the Red Book, Blue Book, or the National Automobile Dealers Association Black Book.

Books, such as the *Used Car Price Guide* published by Pace Publications of Milwaukee, Wisconsin, supplies helpful price information. This publication comes out six times annually.

Another good source is *Best Buys in Used Cars* by Jim Mateja (Bonus Books, Inc., Chicago, 1995). It's lively reading and contains a lot of hard-hitting facts that you won't find elsewhere.

Once you know your car's value you can contact dealers, place classified ads or offer it to a friend.

FURNITURE: IDENTIFICATION & CARE

The largest household pieces you will sell are your furniture. First walk around the house and just look. What do you actually want to sell? Next, write down the pieces you have decided to sell. List the name—such as sofa—age—perhaps 20 years old—and condition. How many pieces have you listed to sell? Mark an "A" before antique pieces, an "O" for old pieces and a "U" for upholstered ones. The upholstered 20-year-old sofa might be part of a house sale, while your great-grandma's sideboard might do better at auction. You have to sort and separate. It's easier if you list the pieces by room or by definition such as antique, old, upholstered, un-upholstered or metal.

Next, get a handle on current prices. Is that old sofa in the basement—the one with the curved arms—an early 19th-century piece? Do you know they go for $1,000 to $7,000 routinely? Blanket chests from Pennsylvania often fetch over $4,000, Windsor chairs from the 18th century from $1,000 to over $5,000. While an old set of "in the style of" dining room chairs might be worth only $35 each, a nice 20th-century walnut chest might bring $1,500, and so on. It all adds up. Especially when you add other residential items such as silver, china, art, books, or jewelry. Don't downgrade in your mind what your possessions are worth. One good sale with additional smaller ones may happily surprise you.

Can you identify the style of your furniture? Do you know the woods? Once you can identify the pieces you can consult a price guide for ballpark figures. Price guides are useful but cannot tell you exactly what your furniture is worth. They are more successful dealing with particular pieces of depression glass or marked silver. Furniture is not easily priced. Many things, such as condition and style, contribute to the price you may obtain for your furniture. Keep in mind that many similar pieces can go for very different prices. If you sell a piece to a friend, commit it to a house sale, offer it at auction, or sell it to a dealer, the same piece may bring different prices. Obviously, timing plays a key role. A piece will bring more when the market is high or if that type of piece was recently featured in a national magazine. If your area is depressed, objects may sell for low prices.

Certain auction houses do better with country pieces. Others successfully sell "in the style of." That is why you must check out more than one auction house. Ask for records of recent sales.

Then think it through. Ask yourself: Do you require an appraiser? Should you call in an auction house? A house sale person? Offer things to your family? Would contacting a dealer be best? Do you want to donate the whole caboodle to a charity?

Go slow. Take one piece at a time and consider the best place to offer it for sale.

Study your lists. Do you have your new or newer pieces and upholstered ones listed? What about wicker furniture? You should check out antique shops that specialize in this furniture. Use your phone book. Dealers have customers for this type of furniture. American wicker made "in the style" and "of the period" of Victorian furniture is a unique art form. Although these pieces are valuable, some are left in alleys for garbage pickup.

Lamps often get lost along the way. Even antique lamps do not always fetch great prices, but if each is sold carefully, the money adds up. Antique lamps might go to auction while merely old ones might do fine at a house sale. (Check lamps in the Question and Answer chapter.)

Now comes decision time. Have you decided what you will sell and what you cannot part with, such as your mother's dressing table? Fine. Don't sell anything you will regret giving up. Where to sell is the next step.

If you are ready to call an auction house, be sure to contact more than one. After talking to them you can decide if an auction sale will serve your purposes for some things or for everything.

Also consider calling a house sale service. If you have a house sale, you probably will include many objects such as costume jewelry, linens, mirrors, toys, bric-a-brac and perhaps books. I recommend you check these items thoughtfully to be sure they are not extremely valuable before lumping them together. Many bargains are found at house sales by "pickers." You, however, do not want to be the "picked." By getting more than one opinion you protect yourself. Everyone is not "up front." There are house sale people that arrange for their relatives to walk off with something *they* need. Use people with a good track record. Check them out with your local chamber of commerce. If you have only a few pieces, a house sale person can incorporate them into another sale.

If you want to sell top of the line traditional mahogany furniture, e.g., Baker, Kittinger, Beacon Hill, Robert Irwin, Kindal, you might check the ads in *Arts and Antiques Magazine.*

Acquiring things can be fun. But disposing of them can be a headache. Keep your monetary goal in focus. Don't dump things because you're tired. If the grand piano has to go, start with the yellow pages in the phone book. Ask your piano tuner if he knows a good place to sell it. Have it tuned before you offer it for sale. Check with auction houses. Check ads in your local newspaper under musical instruments. If you would like to give it to a grandchild, have your son or daughter arrange for it to be picked up and delivered to their house. Get started. Once you make the first decision the others will fall into line.

Handle each piece with care. Do not bump, nick, leave wet glasses on, scratch or in any manner damage the pieces. Condition is important! Books like *Refurbishing Antiques* by Rosemary Ratcliff can aid you with simple restorations. Fine pieces should not be worked on by an amateur.

Every piece with drawers needs one extra effort. You should remove each drawer and feel behind them. Many important documents, military records, birth certificates, World War II ration books, report cards, post cards, union cards, draft cards, land agreements and old letters may have worked their way behind the drawers. Sometimes these finds are historically important. Local historical societies are interested in such material. A photo of yourself as a young child with your family can be a heartwarming find. The stamps on old envelopes are also collectible. Even prize ribbons work behind drawers, as well as paper money and jewelry. Be sure to look. You might need a flashlight.

What constitutes proper furniture care? Concerning humidity, if you are comfortable, your furniture also will be comfortable. What about waxing? Not more than twice a year with a fine paste wax. No sprays or liquids. Dust with a soft cloth when cleaning. Do not damage your pieces. Do not put porous clay such as a pottery pot with plants or flowers on your furniture.

Furniture Woods

Recognizing furniture wood simplifies the disposal process. Furniture woods are not always easy to identify. Even museums often place a question mark on their card files. A mahogany dresser will probably be more valuable than a maple one. Identifying the wood can tell you the origin of the piece. Knowing styles is also important. Books can help. My four: *How to Speak Furniture with an Antique American Accent, How to Speak Furniture with an Antique Victorian Accent, How to Speak Furniture with an Antique English Accent,* and *How to Speak Furniture with an Antique French Accent,* published by Bonus Books, Chicago, IL, deal with style, design and vocabulary.

Oak. This wood has a straight grain and can be steamed and bent to a rounded shape. Oak was used for making English and European furniture since the early periods. American oak was also used in the making of early colonial furniture. They are different in that American oak furniture retains its golden tones while English oak darkens. Old English oak pieces like Windsor chairs have a coarse, raised grain that you can feel with your fingertips. Oak regained its importance in the Victorian period. Many fine Arts and Crafts pieces were made of oak.

Mahogany. This is a strong tropical wood. Beginning in the 16th century it was used to build ships. The finest timbers came from Cuba. Today mahogany is considered the ideal cabinet wood. Its color ranges from yellowish or pinkish tones to deep reddish or purplish brown. Mahogany has plain figures and swirl grains. Its timbers display fine stripes and elliptical markings, fiddle-back, mottle, blister and may have dark flakes called roe. Mahogany does not gray from exposure to sunlight as walnut does. It also carves well. Mahogany stained a deep reddish color originates from the Empire period in France and America. A dark mahogany piece was probably polished with oil, as polishing with wax results in a lighter tone.

Walnut. This wood is used for all types of furniture. American walnut is considered superior to European walnut because it can withstand the furniture beetle. American walnut is moderately hard and more difficult to work with than the European walnut. It has markings of stripe and mottle. Irregular growths, crooks, forks, stumps and burls still produce prized veneers. Walnut is browner than mahogany. Red walnut ages to brandy hues. Victorian black walnut was achieved by applying a stain or acid to walnut which had any red tinges. It then turned dark.

Satinwood. This comes from the East Indies and Ceylon. It belongs to the mahogany family. It is a hard but brittle wood that varies from light to dark golden tones. It is lustrous and takes a fine polish. It is too brittle for large pieces and is primarily used for cross-banding. Some English chairs and continental furniture, however, were made entirely from this wood. American furniture makers often stained birch to resemble satinwood. In the American Federal period birch was used to imitate satinwood for inlay.

Maple. This was commonly used as a primary wood in American colonial furniture. It is strong and hard with a straight grain. As it ages, maple becomes browner, ultimately becoming rich and honey colored. Maple can be easily confused with birch and cherry. All three can look alike when stained. Timbers containing bird's-eye, stripe and curl markings are highly prized. Maple timbers weigh less than cherry timbers.

Rosewood. This is found in Brazil and Madagascar. Its color ranges yellowish-tan to deeper orangish-red to a very dark purplish color. It has brownish or black pigment figures and may have ivory streaks. Rosewood was highly sought after in the late 18th century and the early 19th century. Wonderful pieces were made in the Empire and Victorian periods. It remains an important furniture wood today.

Yew wood. A softwood native of England, yew is often confused with fruitwoods because of its orangish color similar to the American red cedar. American furniture was not made of yew.

Pear wood. A fruitwood with no figure, pear finishes to a light brown. Many fine country pieces have been made of pear in America and Europe.

Cherry wood. Cherry, American black or wild cherry grows all through the eastern half of America, except in southern Florida. It is reddish-brown, moderately hard and has a straight grain. On various timbers a simple ring growth can be found. On rare occasions swirl, feather, or wavy figures are evident. During colonial times, black cherry was used in the states north of Pennsylvania and New Jersey. In New England and New York, cherry wood was used to make some of the finest pieces including highboys, lowboys, secrétaires and chests. It was also used for revival pieces. Cherry pieces continue to be appreciated, especially in Early American styles.

Pine wood. This is quite a hard wood with a definite grain. When finished, it is a light brown color. Northern yellow pine, which was used for Early American pieces, is now extinct. White pine—called pumpkin pine—is a soft wood but with a straight grain. When this pine is finished, it can be a yellow to light amber color. White pine was frequently used for back boards and bottoms on case pieces, drawer slides, and for painted pieces. White pine scars easily and can brown or blacken from years of waxing. It can also bleach or whiten from years of scrubbing, as a kitchen table. Southern pine is a strong, rather hard wood with a definite grain of clear and pitch and takes a good polish. When finished, it is a light brown with reddish pitch stripes. Pine furniture has often been used for painted pieces. Early English and Irish pine cupboards are now collector items.

Birch wood. This is a yellow, very hard and close-grained wood that takes a high polish. Its grain is similar to maple but heavier. The finished color is light brown to amber. Birch can be stained to resemble other woods.

Native woods were usually used for making early French furniture, such as oak, walnut or local fruitwoods. The French also imported ebony and purple wood. Rosewood, mahogany, satinwood, knot-elm and beech were also important. Maple and lemon woods were often used for bedroom pieces.

Some price ranges for furniture:

Georgian era mahogany side chairs, Chippendale style, set of four–$1,276.

Nineteenth-century library secrétaire bookcase–$25,000.

Federal inlaid mahogany mirror, 1790-1810–$10,350.

A Louisiana cherry and walnut armoire–$1,320.

Edwardian kidney-shaped desk–$4,675.

A contemporary Georgian-style mahogany cabinet-on-chest–$316.

A mahogany serpentine chest, perhaps Newport, Rhode Island–$20,000.

A long, painted, wood box with traces of old red paint–$400.

A mid-18th-century painted armchair from Pennsylvania–$4,600.

A Victorian footstool with a velvet rolling pin rest–$200.

An American Federal period country desk–$1,700.

A painted pie safe–$3,350.

An old Connecticut rocker–$675.

An American Gothic-style, circa 1840, mahogany armoire–$2,475.

A late 19th-century painted cast-iron bench–$1,150.

A Hepplewhite slant-front desk–$1,100.

A Sheraton bedside table with two drawers–$440.

A country Hepplewhite cherry nightstand, circa 1870–$385.

Three Charles and Ray Eames chairs from 1950s–$1,092 at auction. (A single one at a house sale–seven dollars.)

A Louis XV-style commode, circa 1900–$4,400.

An oak hall stand from the 1900s with a beveled mirror–$650.

An Italian Renaissance-style, 19th-century corner chair–$660.

A Gustav Stickley side chair from 1907–$250.

A one-piece poplar, comb-grained corner cupboard, some damage, 19th century–$700.

Giltwood 19th-century sofa, French–$4,675.

An Elizabethan-style oak and parcel gilt cupboard, second half of 19th century–$1,100.

A George III mahogany slant-front desk, early 19th century–$1,500.

A Stuart oak blanket chest–$1,800.

A Regency carved walnut commode, first quarter 19th century–$3,200.

A Biedermeier-style oak clothes press–$2,600.

A Mission-style oak china cabinet by L & J.G. Stickley–$3,220.

An Eames rocker of molded fiberglass, manufactured by Herman Miller, circa 1950–$415.

A Philadelphia Centennial Chippendale highboy–$2,145.

Country pine drop-front secretary–$2,145.

Stickley Brothers sideboard–$1,705.

Wallace Nutting single drawer tavern table in tiger maple–$770.

Set of six red and gold painted rush-seated chairs–$3,550.

Rococo Revival card table, mahogany–$700.

Rococo Revival rosewood dresser with marble top–$900.

Hand-caned settee, mahogany, circa late 19th or early 20th–$605.

Pennsylvania cherry corner cupboard–$7,475.

Gumwood two-part linen press–$3,105.

Tiger maple Connecticut Bonnet chest-on-chest–$34,500.

Chippendale mahogany piecrust table–$12,075.

New York rosewood side cabinet branded *G. Herter*–$8,250.

Five-piece Rococo Revival parlor suite–$5,500.

ORIENTAL RUGS

Oriental rugs are usually sold to a dealer or through an auction house. Do not allow a dealer to walk in your home and just walk out with your rugs. First you must have an idea of their worth. Call an appraiser that deals primarily in carpets. Look in your phone book under Appraisal Societies. They can recommend a specialist. Hire one. Oriental rugs can be tricky. Condition, age, type and size will affect the price.

The rug market is softer than in former years, but many orientals still command excellent prices. An auction house with a carpet department is a good choice. Use a reserve—an order that does not allow the piece to be sold for under a recorded amount. You don't want to give your rugs away. Should you decide to clean them, check with an auction house or a respected dealer. Don't harm them by using an unskilled person.

Always try to find out the most recent prices. Write to two or more auction houses for their last carpet sale catalogue and the realized prices. It's worth the cost. Recently, a silk Kashan sold for $14,500. Its low estimate was $1,000. See how valuable auctioning can be?

Christie's, Skinner's and Sotheby's auction houses do well by fine rugs. Leslie Hindman in Chicago is another excellent house.

Star Kazak, worn–$17,250.

Lori Pombak Kazak–$8,050.

Ottoman Cairene–$123,500.

Sultanabad–$27,600.

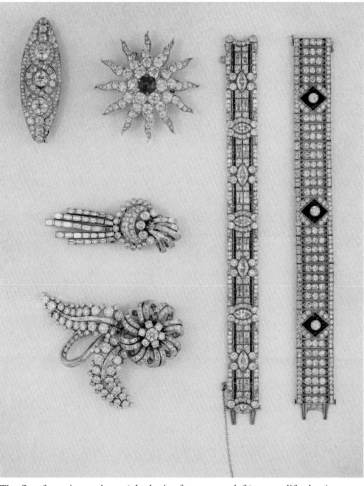

The first four pieces above (clockwise from upper left) exemplify the Art
Deco style of the '20s, while the fifth and sixth pieces date back to the '40s.
All of these pieces contain diamonds and platinum with the exception of the
second piece, a brooch, which is made up of yellow gold and a sapphire
center. 1994-95 auction values (clockwise from upper left): 1) $15,000
2) signed "Tiffany" $15,000 3) $40,000 4) $25,000 5) $15,000 6) $7,000.

Art Nouveau gold brooch, circa 1899, four repoussé cherubs within a gold frame highlighted with pink and green enamel flowers and vines, relief by E. Becker (minor enamel loss), valued at $5,170.

Bottom left corner: Bakelite "Toastmaster" pin valued at $695. Other pins in this group are of comparable values, circa 1930, approx. 4" tall.

"Star of Bethlehem" pattern quilt, circa 1830, 114" x 116", valued at $9,200.

Kashan Oriental rug, circa 1900, 4' 2" x 7' 10", valued at $14,500.

Paul Emil Jacobs (German 1802-1866), oil on canvas, "Judith and Holofernes," 59" x 48" — $33,350.

Arthur Grover Rider
(American), watercolor,
"Spanish Coastal
Scene," 10" x 14",
valued at $6,325.

courtesy of Dunnings

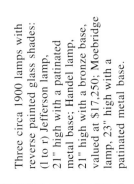

Three circa 1900 lamps with reverse painted glass shades: (l to r) Jefferson lamp, 21" high with a patinated metal base; Handel lamp, 21" high with a bronze base, valued at $17,250; Moebridge lamp, 23" high with a patinated metal base.

courtesy of *Leslie Hindman*

German blown glass and etched goblets, 18th century, valued between $300 and $800.

Nineteenth century French bronze clock with porcelain face, valued at $21,160.

Pair of terrestrial and celestial globes on mahogany stands, circa 1850, by Thomas Malby and Son, fair condition, valued at $12,650.

Nineteenth century library secretaire bookcase attributed to the Herter Brothers, originally from George Pullman House; ebonized cherry, light cherry marquetry borders and bronze embossing, 12' 7" wide, 6' 3" tall; $25,000.

Georgian mahogany breakfront secretary bookcase, upper section having four gothic-style glazed doors, 87" tall, 84" wide; $13,555.

A Los Castillo mixed metal pitcher with green
enameled parrot handle, 13" high, valued at
$517.50.

A Picasso round terre de faience plate, circa 1963;
glazed, painted in blue, red, yellow, green, and black;
numbered 297/500 on the bottom and inscribed
Madoura and *Edition Picasso*; valued between $1,200
and $1,600.

Platinum and diamond necklace, designed as a slightly graduated row of eighteen pear-shaped diamonds, approx. total wt. 16.00 cts.; suspended from an undulating baguette-cut diamond mount, approx. total wt. 11.75 cts.; enhanced by clusters of round diamonds, approx. total wt. 15.00 cts.; 18" long, valued between $35,000-$45,000.

Tekke Mafrash–$10,350.

Ushah–$32,000.

Baluch–$9,200.

Shirvan–$21,850.

Heriz (palace size)–$112,500.

Shiraz–$2,200.

Heriz–$6,400.

An excellent book on carpets is *Oriental Carpets in the Philadelphia Museum* by Charles Ellis. Also see *The Official Price Guide to Oriental Rugs* by Joyce Ware, but be aware that the prices have changed since 1992 when the book was published.

ART

Art is a special category encompassing paintings, sculpture and works on paper, such as prints and collages.

The first thing you must know is "what is it." Is the piece an original oil painting? Is it an original print? Is it signed by the artist? Has it been repainted, restored, or over-cleaned? When was it created? Is there any documentation? Is the sculpture original or a reproduction? What material is it made of such as stone, marble, metal, wood, etc.? Is it signed? Do you have an insurance appraisal on the piece? You can't sell responsibly unless you know what you have to sell.

Get a current market value of the piece before you contact auction houses or dealers. A local museum in your area might authenticate pieces of art. Some museums will authenticate but they will not give prices. Often you have to be a member of the musem. If you believe your piece to be the work of a major artist, calling a musem is a good idea. Always contact the proper department based on the category of your art. Leave a message. Someone will probably call you back. Every bit of knowledge you garner will aid you. Write down everything you learn and who you learned it from. Knowledge is money!

If you see a signature on a painting or print you do not recognize, that does not mean the artist is not important. Visit your library. Most libraries have reference books giving the names of "listed" artists and their signatures. A listed artist is one that has had shows or won awards. There are separate volumes for American and European artists with their signatures. You can also use a museum library to look up artists. The Chicago Art Institute is one I frequent. You have to sign in, as such libraries have many valuable books on their shelves. They also have current art price lists in books such as *Gordons Price Guide*.

If you don't want to do the research yourself, you might call an art appraiser or an auction house. Look in the phone book for appraisal societies and ask for the name of an expert for your type of art. Or call museums and ask if they might recommend an expert. At this point you can go back to the museum library for additional information about the artist and the period. They have books listing international and national prices—by year—of the works of major artists. The print is small in these volumes, so bring your reading glasses. For a small fee museums will xerox information and mail it to you.

Whether you are selling one work or a collection, you must know exactly what you have. Never assume. Do not believe verbal information that you may have been given. Your parents or friends, for example, may or may not be accurate. You must know the facts. Many people think they own an original, but it turns out to be a reproduction. Others assume a work to be a reproduction because it did not cost much. Many original pieces sold for small amounts when first purchased. An original Toulouse-Lautrec poster that sold for a few dollars in the 1890s and a few hundred in 1950s can be worth over $40,000 today. Valuable art cannot be judged by the size of its gold frame or the cheapness of its black frame. Once I found an original Jules Pascin drawing on crumbled wrapping paper stuck in a dime store frame at a junky show of repro Victorian furniture.

Your idea of what is beautiful is also not valid. Ugly does not mean invaluable. Many times an appraiser will discover marvelous art work by accident, having come to appraise another piece. Have everything checked by an expert if possible.

Works on paper that are under glass must be unframed to examine properly. No self-respecting appraiser will price art unless they examine the piece out of the frame.

If you have a modern print, it will probably be numbered to show how many images were made from the original plate. The exception is an artist's proof—one or more prints the artist pulled before beginning to number the edition. Often the artist's proof was a working proof, meaning the work was still in progress, and therefore not numbered. Prints with large numbers are usually not as valuable as those with a small edition. Proofs were often given as gifts by the artist. Unfortunately, famous artists such as Dali have had their work forged and sold as original with dealers putting fake numbers on them. Appraisers and auction houses keep lists of suspect prints.

Old prints were only signed on the plate. Newer prints are usually signed by the artist on the plate and on the print itself, by hand. Some prints carry false signatures that were forged to increase the prints' value. False signatures appear on all types of art, so the more valuable a piece may be, the more wary the expert must be. Some forgers do not even try to imitate the actual signature. They are just written on the piece. These are easy to spot.

Dealers have even sold prints that appeared in magazines as original prints. This is another reason to take them out of the frame. Old prints that originally appeared in magazines may be original lithographs by important artists. Although they have print on their reverse side, these may be valuable—not as valuable as an original print made to sell as a separate print would be—however, particular collectors cherish these old pieces.

Until recent scientific advances exposed them, many museums unknowingly hung some forgeries.

Timing really is everything. If you are lucky and smart, you might sell at the top of the market. Good timing determines this. If an artist is becoming well known or you think this might happen, perhaps you should wait. If you hear a museum is planning a retrospective of an artist whose work you have, perhaps you should hold out until the show is on. The art market is like the stock market. Prices fluctuate. For that reason some sellers would rather sell to a dealer than take a chance at auction.

Today's art market has not reached the highs achieved in the 1980s. People that bought at the height of the market and now want to sell are discovering this. Many dealers implied the art would go up X% each year. Unfortunately, they only implied, but some buyers believed this would happen. Many pieces may never sell for what the last owner paid for them. Sometimes size can play a role. When collectors wanted a "picture wall," many small pictures were acquired. Now the trend is to larger pieces that make a different statement.

Art collectors are buying new categories such as south-western and Latin American, cutting into former markets.

The condition of pieces will reflect their sale price. I continually see oil paintings that have been poorly cleaned, leaving them poster-like with their shadow areas flat. It is better not to touch artwork unless a museum or art expert recommends a particular craftsman. Sadly, many of the people that clean their paintings are delighted with the results. They show me the work and proudly tell me they now look new. Proper restoration is also an art, but bad restoration is terrible! Prints, too, may be worked on. When buying, you need to study them carefully to see if areas have been touched up. If a work is torn or foxed, it can be restored beautifully. I have had pieces restored at the Kenyon Gallery in Chicago by Joel Oppenheim. They look wonderful. Hopefully, your artworks have not been exposed to the sun or been matted with mats that are not acid free. Faded artwork loses much of its value, but UV glass can protect it from light. Ceramic or marble pieces that are chipped reflect their defects at market. Condition is important!

Then go to your local library. Look at *Arts and Antiques Magazine* and other fine art magazines for dealer ads listing the artists they are searching for. You may own exactly what they want to purchase. For instance, Roughton Galleries say they are interested in 19th- and early 20th-century European, English and American artists, (214) 871-1096. If you have any, why not give them a call? Or the Green River Gallery is currently buying American 19th- and 20th-century art, (518) 789-3311, Byron and Sons Gallery is looking for Indiana artists, (317) 923-1285, and Philippine paintings are requested, (800) 654-2017.

While art is mainly sold by auction and dealers, it is also sold with the use of newsletters. *The Art Collector's Quarterly* [860 Cedar Lane, Northbrook, Illinois 60662, (708) 564-1660] is an agent in the form of a newsletter. The format and artwork descriptions are very similar to that of an auction catalogue. It is another means by which an individual can safely and discreetly sell artworks. Both dealers and collectors may utilize this newsletter. Selling prices can be negotiated. The seller is not required to give up possession of the artwork until he is comfortable with the conditions of the sale. The prices are researched. Elaine Kwan, the founder of *The Art Collectors Quarterly*, has been an art collector and dealer for over 20 years and uses the latest in computer communication and information retrieval. This is another avenue to explore.

Some recent art prices:

An oil canvas by Marguerite Stuber Pearson, 1898-1978, signed and dated, 26" x 22", titled *Venus and Fruit*–$4,900.

An unsigned *Madonna and Child*, oil–$6,600.

A Norman Rockwell *Freedom of Speech*, illustration–$407,000.

A Picasso gouache over pencil on charcoal–$2.84 million.

A Picasso ceramic plaque–$2,200.

An early Jackson Pollock sketch–$15,000.

A Georgia O'Keeffe *Jimson Weed*–$1,047,500.

A Joan Miro lithograph on vinyl, titled *Interior and Night*–$3,800.

A Louis Icart drypoint and aquatint–$1,700.

A Jean Dubuffet lithograph–$2,200.

A Lynn Chadwick bronze sculpture–$8,200.

An Antoine Louis Barye cast metal sculpture–$200.

A Japanese scroll, 18th or 19th century, on silk–$1,100.

An Edward Curtis photogravure–$350.

A Kiyoshi Saito wood cut–$400.

Susan Watkins, *Woman in a French Interior*, 1908–$76,750.

American School, *Portrait of an Indian*–$33,350.

Frederic S. Remington, *The Cheyenne*, bronze–$63,000.

John Audubon, *Wild Ducks Rising*, 1840–$96,000.

Ben Shahn, *Three Men*, 1939–$93,250.

Stuart Davis, *Marine Landscape*, 1937–$32,200.

Harriet Frishmuth, *Jay of the Waters*, sculpture–$27,000.

JEWELRY

A lifetime of owned or inherited jewelry will produce varied results. There might be a diamond engagement ring and matching band, a plain gold wedding ring, inherited pieces from deceased relatives, birthday and Christmas jewelry consisting of pearls, gold, silver, watches, necklaces, brooches, pins and many costume pieces. Fashion in jewelry constantly changes. Victorian jewelry set with glass stones, once discarded, is now highly desirable and is even shown at museums, such as the Victoria and Albert in London. Diamond stud earrings, once the mainstay of many women, may now sit in a jewelry box. Large pins are back in style. Large pieces may replace smaller ones, but what goes around also comes around.

People sell their jewelry for many reasons: to settle an estate or because they simply want the money. Others no longer want to own certain pieces. Sometimes people plan to use the money from one sale to buy something they want more. Still others just plan to unburden themselves of things in general. Lifestyles change and so do our needs.

Whether you wish to sell a single piece, such as a ring, or many pieces, it is important to choose your markets with great care.

Jewelry sales can produce large sums of money. Fine jewelry, such as high quality diamond rings, gemstones, antique pieces, estate pieces, gold and platinum, natural and cultured pearls, and even certain wrist watches, are highly desirable. In most circumstances it is not difficult to sell exceptional jewelry. The major auction houses will be happy to handle these valuable pieces. The value of diamonds and other gemstones depend on their size and quality. Dealers are also interested in acquiring fine pieces.

Most jewelry you may own is probably between ordinary

and fantastic. But, like other things you may sell, checks add up to make you wealthier.

Do you have insurance policies on any of the pieces you wish to sell? They can be helpful, not only for prices given, but for detailed descriptions. Prices change, and sale prices will be different than replacement prices, but descriptions can provide style, size, weight, stones, metal, gold content, etc.

Examine each piece carefully. Use a magnifying glass to check for type of gold (14K or 18K) usually imprinted on the piece, or the name of the designer or manufacturer of the piece. Can you identify the gems or stones incorporated in the pieces? Do you know approximately when the pieces were made?

It is worth your time to give both the auction house and private dealers a careful look. In an auction, be sure that many similar pieces will be offered. This way many buyers will see your pieces. Request recent sale prices of like items from the auction houses beforehand. Always consult more than one auction house. You can call, send photographs, talk to the resident expert, take the pieces to the auction house for appraisal and negotiate for the best deal you can make. It never hurts to ask for more than you expect.

Take various pieces to a dealer that handles the sale of estate pieces and other secondary sales. Before you commit to any one dealer, be absolutely sure they have a good reputation and have been in business many years. Check them out with the Better Business Bureau. Do not open your phone book and pick the dealer with the largest ad. After initial phone contact they will probably want photographs and then request an appointment to see the pieces. Out-of-town dealers may want you to send them the pieces to examine. Many people are not comfortable with this arrangement, although it is frequently done. Of course, the jewelry must be insured if mailed. Some dealers are willing to meet you at your bank to examine particular pieces. This is the safest way. Some dealers will buy pieces outright, while others work on consignment.

Whatever arrangements you make, get them in writing. Don't be concerned with taking up the dealers' time.

Before you sign anything, read the contract slowly and carefully. Be certain you understand the terms.

If your jewelry was created by a name designer, it will bring a higher price. For instance, a Tiffany necklace will bring more money than a similar necklace made by a lesser known company. These signed pieces are referred to as "pedigree pieces."

If you own damaged jewelry, it is better to sell it as jewelry rather than for its metal or gem value. Craftsmen can repair basically good pieces and dealers know and use these people before reselling your pieces.

As with every type of object, pieces that are currently popular bring higher prices, such as fine Art Deco or Georgian pieces.

Coin jewelry will not be as valuable as the coins would have been if left loose. Once coins have been incorporated into jewelry, they lose their value and are simply sold as jewelry.

Watches can be very valuable. The solid gold pocket watch is still highly appreciated by collectors. Usually watches are 9–14K or merely plated. The jewels in the watch also affect the value. A watch person knows the difference and can give you a current price. Pocket watches with their original fobs and chains are more valuable.

Wrist watches can also be valuable. Pedigree name watches are very desirable. Names such as Piaget, Vacheron, Universal, Geneve, Audemans, Brequet, Cartier, Corum, and Ebel will ring a collector's bell. A book to consult is *Vintage American and European Book of Wrist Watches* by Sherry and Roy Ehrhardt and Joe De Mesy.

The in-between pieces can be the more difficult to sell. After discovering whether an auction house might be interested, you can also take another route. Attend antique shows, mall and church sales of antiques and collectibles where a great deal of jewelry is sold. Check the newspaper for the listing of sales. There is almost never a weekend without some sale going on. Talk to dealers handling like pieces. Carry photographs to show. Some people simply take their jewelry with them to sales. Dealers are always looking for merchandise. Most dealers do many shows rather than pay rent for a shop. Check the asking prices for similar jewelry to determine if you are being offered a fair price. Remember, the dealer has to make a profit so you will not be offered the retail price. If you have a large amount of jewelry, a dealer might buy everything. So don't dump jewelry that you think isn't valuable into a drawer. Checks add up and people are surprised how much money can be had from old or costume pieces. House or garage sales have brisk jewelry sales. Take care of everything.

Opals and pearls should not be placed in airtight plastic bags as they need air. Pearls can stain so don't place them near perfume, cosmetics or dyed materials. Diamonds can scratch other diamonds and all gem stones, so keep them separate. If you have original boxes, hold onto them. They enhance the piece. Again, don't jumble up jewelry. You may dent, scratch or break them.

If your opals look faded, very lightly apply vaseline to the stone and wrap it gently in a soft cloth. Leave it for a few months and then, like magic, it will glow with renewed brilliant color.

Stone cameos are more valuable than the shell cameos.

Brilliant imperial green jade is very valuable. Carved jade pieces are not as valuable as cabochon pieces. Jade comes in many colors such as: brown, cinnabar red, lavender, black, white, yellow and many shades of green. Spinach green with golden glints is rare. Homogenic jade—less mottled—is more valuable. People seldom sell such jade pieces. They pass them onto the next generation, sometimes preferring them to diamonds. The Aztecs and Mayans regarded jade as divine and the Maoris of New Zealand believed jade had magical powers.

Valuable pearls are either natural or cultured. Glass pearls that appear on costume pieces are not valuable. The only sure way to tell if your pearls are natural or cultured is to have them x-rayed. The natural pearl will have grains of sand in its center, while the cultured ones will show a bead that was inserted into the oyster. Oyster or pearl farming is a big business. Natural black pearls from the South Seas command high prices. Some experts bite gently to feel for the certain roughness of a natural pearl. Still, I advise keeping your teeth off your pearls and having them x-rayed!

The New York Times regularly runs ads listing important auction jewelry sales. They provide information on the auction house (e.g. William Doyle) as well as offering catalogues for sale. Watch for these advertisements. Write down the names, addresses, phone and fax numbers of these important auction houses. Write away for catalogues that pertain to your pieces. The catalogues will also give you a working jewelry vocabulary.

The basic shape of jewelry stones are: round, square, triangle, octagon, keystone, lozenge, pentagon, hexagon, oval, pear, and heart.

There is an amazing amount of costume jewelry around. Some of it is very collectible. Other pieces will sell for whatever you can get. Name pieces are the most collectible and valuable. Though many prices tumbled by as much as one-third in 1993 and early in 1994 after nine years of gains, the collectible costume jewelry market is staging a comeback.

A 1950s HAR snake bracelet worth five dollars 10 years ago, now–$350.

A 1950s Nettie Rosenstein tremblant dragonfly brooch–$230.

A 1960s Kenneth Jay Lane choker with beads and rhinestones–$200.

A swan-shape Trifari brooch–$5,000.

A Bakelite cherry necklace worth $50 in 1985–$200–$300.

Names such as Hobe, Eisenberg, Weiss, Givenchy, Christian Dior, Miriam Haskell, Boucher, Schiaparelli, Rosenstein, Hattie Carnegie, Trifari, Monet, Ciher, Kramer of New York, Coro and Mazer are sought after.

Gerald A. Browne's novel *18mm Blues*, published by Time Warner, is perfect for readers with an interest in adventure and gems.

H. Horwitz Co. (Water Tower Place, 845 North Michigan Avenue, Chicago, Illinois) is a dealer who purchases estate jewelry.

Some jewelry prices:

A triangular brooch, French, circa 1935, from the collection of Coco Chanel, set with cushion-cut rubies, emeralds, sapphires and diamonds–$51,750.

A pendant brooch from the collection of Sonia Henie, cabochon ruby and diamonds–$29,900.

An Art Deco opal and diamond bracelet from the 1920s–$10,637.

An enamel and diamond brooch, centered by an oval blue enamel plaque, highlighted by a rose-cut diamond from the mid-19th century–$373.

Art Deco platinum diamond and coral ring–$1,100.

Antique gem-set pansey pin in 18K yellow gold–$2,990.

Edwardian platinum and enamel pendant watch–$1,092.

Japanese Shakudo pin with 14K yellow gold mount–$258.

Art Deco 14K yellow gold and black enamel compact–$1,150.

Gentleman's Oyster "Bubbleback" watch, circa 1937, with Mercedes hands by Rolex–$2,800.

Gentleman's 18K yellow gold watch by Brequet–$7,800.

Gentleman's 18K white gold Ebel wrist watch–$5,400.

Lady's platinum and diamond brooch containing 49 full cut diamonds–$13,500.

Pair of lady's 18K yellow gold and diamond earclips containing 74 assorted full cut diamonds–$3,600.

Lady's four-strand cultured pearl necklace containing 9.50 mm–10.0 mm cultured pearls–$5,000.

Lady's 14K yellow and white gold and diamond ring containing one pear shape diamond weighing approximately 1.60 carats–$4,000.

Lady's 14K yellow gold diamond and ruby brooch–$1,600.

Lady's 14K yellow and white gold multi-chain necklace–$170.

Two pairs of lady's 14K yellow gold earrings–$70.

Pair of gentleman's 14K yellow gold and moonstone cufflinks–$550.

Lady's nine-strand, dark angel skin, coral bead necklace–$225.

Lady's gold-filled bracelet–$60.

BOOKS

Books are often overlooked in selling residential contents. Most people don't keep track of book prices, but it is possible to generate more money from books than from your valued china.

My husband and I recently sold thirteen books for $1,000. Only one was old and it needed rebinding. The others were novels by well-known authors, no older than 30 years, first editions, in excellent condition, and *with their original dust jackets*.

Saving original dust jackets can not be stressed enough. If a book is worth $200 with its dust jacket, it will probably be worth only $10 without it.

The biggest problem with selling books is their weight. Sorting, packing and perhaps mailing is heavy work. Still, go through your library and sort by topic—fiction, non-fiction—first editions, and condition. Children's books have recently become desirable to collectors. Do not simply donate books to whatever organization will pick them up. But certainly give the leftovers to organizations and libraries and obtain a tax form for them.

Second, decide how to best sell them. Contact book dealers or call an auction house. If you have very valuable books, try an auction house, such as Swann in New York, that specializes in rare books.

If you know in advance that you will be selling your books, go to book fairs. There you can meet book dealers, each with a specialty. Check prices yourself to get an idea of what your books are worth. It's time-consuming but interesting. Book dealers are interesting people in themselves and you might enjoy knowing many of them on a personal level. Dealers we have bought from or sold to are now friends first and dealers second.

The yellow pages of your local phone book can provide the names and phone numbers of dealers and auction houses.

Books must usually be first editions (printings), and are subject to condition factors. These prices indicate what a dealer, such as Tom Joyce of J. Joyce and Company, Chicago, would pay, *not retail price*.

Listed below is a selection of authors, titles and subjects that might be of interest:

Baum, L. Frank, *The Wonderful Wizard of Oz*, George M. Hill: Chicago, 1900–$1,500.

Carroll, Lewis, *Alice's Adventures in Wonderland*. Large book-shaped box containing text with 13 plates by Salvador Dali, including one signed by him–$1,000.

Chagall, Marc, *The Jerusalem Windows*, New York or Monte Carlo, 1962–$500.

Cushing, Harvey, *The Life of Sir William Osler, M.D.*, two volumes, Oxford, 1925–$150.

Doyle, Arthur Conan, *The Sign of Four*, New York, 1891, published in P.F. Collier's Once a Week Library–$1,000.

Du Bois, W.E.B., *The Souls of Black Folk*, McClurg: Chicago, 1903–$250.

Einstein, Albert, *Albert Einstein: Philosopher–Scientist*, Library of Living Philosophers: Evanston, IL, 1949, one of 760 copies signed by Einstein–$1,500.

Ellison, Ralph, *The Invisible Man*, New York, 1952–$250.

Gacy, John Wayne, *A Question of Doubt*, Hannibal, MO, 1993, limited to only 155 numbered copies, each with a letter signed by Gacy–$500.

Gannet, W.C., *The House Beautiful*, Auvergne Press: River Forest, IL, 1896, designed by Frank Lloyd Wright– $1,500.

Grant, U.S., *Personal Memoirs*, two volumes, New York, 1885-6, usually in green cloth, sometimes in brown sheep- skin, or morocco leather spines, apparent autograph is printed facsimile–$50.

Hemingway, Ernest, *The Sun Also Rises*, New York, 1926, first edition, with "stopped" (page 181, line 26) spelled with three p's–$400 (more if dust jacket is present).

Holmes, O.W., Jr., *The Common Law*, Boston, 1881–$250.

Jones, Edith Newbold, *Verses*, Newport, R.I., 1878, poems written by Edith Wharton, published in softcover–$5,000.

Lakeside Classics, one volume per year from 1903-present. Issued by R.R. Donnelley & Co.–five dollars each and upward to several hundred for some of the earlier dates.

Lee, Harper, *To Kill a Mockingbird*, Philadelphia, 1960–$500 (if dust jacket is present).

Mitchell, Margaret, *Gone with the Wind*, New York, 1936, states "Printed May, 1936" on copyright page–$200 (more if original dust jacket present).

Osler, Sir William, M.D., *The Principles and Practice of Medi- cine*, New York, 1892–$250-$500.

Rossetti, Dante Gabriel, *Hand and Soul*, Hammersmith and Chicago, 1895, small book bound in flexible vellum covers– $300.

Salinger, J.D., *Catcher in the Rye*, Boston, 1951, states first edition on copyright page–$500 (if dust jacket present).

Twain, Mark, *The Adventures of Huckleberry Finn*, New York, 1885, bound in green, blue or leather–$500 (more if in original leather binding, or with certain scarcer "points").

Forty-one Waverly novels from the 1830s sold for $280 at auction.

TOYS

This is definitely the time to sell toys. The market is very active. Games, such as Monopoly, in the original box, bring around $1,000. Barbie and Ken dolls, Disney toys, banks, Nancy Ann Storybook dolls, train sets and doll houses are sought after. The market is so hot that reproductions are emerging. If you have authentic pieces, dealers and auction houses will be delighted.

In order to auction off your toys, find an auction house or dealer that specializes in toys. Call around. Do not put toys in an auction with only a few other toys. They would be a steal for a collector. Check newspapers for ads listing toy sales. Call at least four auction houses. They might know of an upcoming toy auction at another house. Do your homework! Check the phone numbers of auction houses in the chapter on auctions. It will pay to ship your toys, if necessary, to another state. Packing services like Mail Boxes Etc. do a good job. Remember to insure your toys before you send them.

Check bedroom shelves, the basement, attic, and the garage for old toys. Are there any china dolls? These sell in the thousands, especially with original period clothes.

Bill Bertoi Auctions [2413 G Madison Ave., Vineland, NJ 08360, (609) 692-1881, fax (609) 692-8697] is an auction house well known for toy sales. Write for a recent catalog. Judith Lile Antique Toys [346 Valleybrook Drive, Lancaster, PA 17601, (717) 569-8175] is another.

Some recent toy prices are:

Buddo the Happy Time Horse, Sears and Roebuck, 1949–$65.

Mickey Mouse pencil holder, J. Dixon, 5"–$75.

Orphan Annie pastry set, Transogram, 1930s–$140.

Dopey musical sweeper, red wood handle–$225.

Quick Draw McGraw, Tiddledy Winks Tennis Game, Milton Bradley, 1961–$435.

Popeye basketball player, lithographed figure, wind-up, Linemar–$1,045.

Howdy Doody ventriloquist doll, 1950s–$135.

Snoopy radio, United Features Syndicate, black and white, carrying strap, made in Hong Kong–$17.

Fisher-Price Molly Moo-Moo, box–$124.

Wolverine Loop-the-Loop rollercoaster–$450.

Steiner doll, Le Parisien, blue paperweight eyes, open mouth, 22"–$2,900.

German bisque Parisienne, Jumeau, circa 1880, swivel head, muslin torso, kid lower arms, provincial costume, 12"–$2,000.

Japanese papier-mâché Ichimatsu doll, circa 1925, sicket head, glass-inset eyes, human hair wig, 24"–$1,550.

French bisque Parisienne by Gaultier, circa 1870, swivel head, kid-lined shoulder plate, mohair wig, over cork pate, kid gusset-joined body, 18"–$2,400.

Tonka truck, allied van, 1950s–$235.

Shirley Temple doll–$250.

Shirley Temple doll buggy–between $400 and $500.

Jumeau bebe doll, circa 1880, bisque head, wood body, 27"–$4,250.

Planters Peanut popgun, circa 1930, folded paper–$220.

Bru bebe doll, Casimir Bru, circa 1885, bisque swivel head on kid lines, bisque shoulder plate with molded breasts and shoulder blades, blue glass paperweight eyes, blond mohair wig over cork plate, wooden lower legs, 27"–$23,000.

Accordion jack-o-lantern, German, circa 1920, cardboard with papier-mâché wash, 8"–$275.

Schoenhuts little wooden toys: Buffalo–$1,100, Acrobat, 8¼"–$286, Camel–$286, African native, two-part head–$2,530 (at a house sale you might get five dollars for these dolls).

Buddy "L" Express truck–$1,100.

Lionel powerhouse–$209.

Standard-gauge Lionel #380 Locomotive–$577.50.

Lionel train set of two locomotives and four cars–$6,600.

Lionel #97 coal elevator with controls and a #206 coal bag–$357.50.

Ives #116 extra-large passenger station with lithographed base–$577.50.

Custom-painted S-gauge American Flyer PA Alco AA–$121.

Standard-gauge Lionel #900 Metropolitan Express boxcar, missing step & handrail–$4,950.

Lionel #763 E Hudson and Tender–$1,760.

Ives cattle car–$1,540.

Dinky #723 Hawker Siddeley executive jets, original box–$55.

Glass candy containers shaped like airplanes–$110, $220, and $94.

STAMPS

Selling a stamp collection is simpler if you have assembled the collection yourself. Collectors are knowledgeable and follow the stamp market. But, if you have acquired a stamp collection through inheritance or gift, you will need information.

As with all types of collections, stamps have their own history and vocabulary. Merely checking out a stamp guide from your library will probably be futile.

First do nothing. Do not disturb the collection. Do not attempt to remove stamps or allow anyone to "play with them." Condition is very important! Next, research a dealer, appraiser or auction house to take them to. Contact the American Philatelic Society or members of the American Stamp Collectors Association who should have current identification cards. Do not deal with persons without the proper credentials. A dealer such as Ned L. Fishkin Ltd. [(312) 641-7397, Chicago, Illinois] can assist you. Mr. Fishkin has been in business for many years buying and selling stamps. He will come to your residence if necessary.

Most dealers do not charge for their appraisal time if you sell them the appraised pieces. If you take your collection elsewhere, you must expect to pay for appraisal time. Ask beforehand what the charge per hour will be. Dealers usually purchase more merchandise prior to Christmas for expected sales.

Dealers will usually pay cash for your collection. Be cautious of giving your collection on consignment even with a contract.

Auction houses are another route. Some will give you an advance on a sale. This will usually take longer than a straight dealer sale because of the time involved until the auction, production of the catalogue and the sale itself. Auction houses charge a commission. Ask what the commission will be. The Rasdale Stamp Company, (312) 263-7334, in Chicago might be a good avenue to pursue.

Check your local phone book, consult with your estate lawyer, or even check dealer listings at your library in books, such as the *Scott Catalogue*. Do not involve friends and family. A professional will offer you the best advice and know how to handle the pieces competently and privately.

COINS

Coin collectors will probably know how to sell their collections if they have kept a current interest in the coin market. However, if you have acquired a collection by gift or inheritance, you will need advice.

Contacting the American Numismatic Association in Colorado Springs, Colorado, should be your first step.

Check with your lawyer, the phone book and dealers listed in coin catalogues that are found at the library. Check with auction houses also. If you plan to use an auction house, check what their commission will be. Also, check their previous sale records. The type of coin may determine your choice. Are they American, European, antique, etc.? Do not remove coins from sealed envelopes. Condition is important! Always be wary of consignment selling, even with a contract.

Always use experts. They can quickly spot rare coins, as well as government reproductions.

Carrying coins about is heavy and dangerous work. You may need assistance or a house appointment, as a collection may be worth a great deal of money. If the collection is stored at a bank, arrange to have an appraisal done there. Do not discuss having a coin collection at home in public. Be discreet!

Some coin prices are:

A pewter 1776 Continental dollar–over $10,000.

An 1830 Liberty dime with no stars–$3,000.

A half eagle gold piece from 1798–$12,000.

Five U.S. St. Gaudens twenty-five dollar gold coins dated 1908, 1909, 1922, 1924, and 1926–$400-$500.

Keep a list of the people you speak with and the information given to you.

Early American Numismatics [P.O. Box 2442, La Jolla, CA 92036, (619) 273-5566, fax (619) 273-3569] and Ned L. Fishkin Ltd. [(312) 641-7397, Chicago, IL] buy colonial American coins and currency notes.

QUESTIONS & ANSWERS

Q. I inherited a gun collection. Where can I sell it?

A. Consider W. M. "Pete" Harvey Gun Auctions [1270 Route 28A, Box 280, Cataumet, MA 02534, (508) 563-2550]. They specialize in firearms.

Q. Where can I sell early photographs?

A. Sotheby's Auction House in New York has an excellent photograph department, (212) 606-7240.

Q. Who buys old maps?

A. Try Ridler Page Rare Maps [203 King St., Charleston, SC 29401, (803) 723-1734].

Q. Where can I sell a fountain pen collection?

A. Pen Fancier's [1169 Overcash Dr., Department M, Dunedin, FL 34698, (813) 734-4742].

Q. What kind of prices do American Indian pieces get?

A. American Indian items are doing very well. A 1925 Sioux hide dress recently fetched $2,875. Southern Plains beaded hide moccasins, $3,335; a pair of northern plains beaded hide moccasins, $6,325; a late classic Navajo wearing blanket for $41,400; a late classic Navajo serape for $17,250; a Chumash basket for $20,700; a Hopi pottery seed jar for $9,200; and a Crow Parfleche bag for $35,650.

Q. Is there a place to sell sailboats?

A. Pond sailers and models, hulls and sails are wanted by Susan P. Meisel Decorative Arts [141 Prince St., New York, NY 10012, (212) 677-1340].

Q. Do you know a music box dealer?

A. Try Marty Roenigk [26 Barton Hill, East Hampton, CT 06424, (203) 267-8682].

Q. Are guitars and banjos worth selling?

A. Of course. Check the phone book yellow pages for dealers. Also consider writing Mandolin Brothers [629 Forest Ave., Staten Island, NY 10310]. You might take them to shops which sell guitars and ask if they are interested. Call an auction house and see if they are having a sale that will feature guitars. Or check ads for guitar trade shows where these instruments are sold and traded.

Q. I have three place settings of china. What can I do with them?

A. Contact various dealers that specialize in replacement patterns. They are listed in phone directories and in magazine ads. They may also be able to complete a set for you. Normally selling three or less place settings is "taking what you can get" unless the china is antique or of rare design. A possible source might be You're Our China Connection, 1-800-562-4462. If you wish to sell one or two place settings of silver, try the As You Like It Silver Shop, 1-800-828-2311.

Q. Can you tell me anything about unmarked pottery?

A. Sometimes pottery is not marked. For example, Roseville made various vases without markings. The workmanship and design can identify these pieces. Call an expert to help you.

Q. I have an Edward VII coronation plate that is eight inches square. Can you tell me what it might be worth?

A. About $45.00 depending on the condition.

Q. I wonder if sheet music, such as Al Jolson's "Oh! How I Wish I Could Sleep Until My Daddy Comes Home" (12" x 9") is worth selling?

A. You could probably get 10 dollars for it. Sheet music in good condition, especially with an attractive cover, is now collectable. Check out shows with dealers that sell them. Sometimes ads are found in collectible magazines requesting such material. Until recently these music sheets were not in demand, but now many collectors search out particular sheets. They are also being framed and hung as a collection.

Q. I read in a newspaper article that milk glass is becoming more popular. I have some and wonder if this is true.
A. Yes. This glass, popular after the Civil War, is back in vogue. Most popular are figural covered dishes. A boar's head covered dish of opalescent milk glass from 1888 is worth $1,800.

Q. I have piles of old records. Can I sell them?
A. Yes. Check your phone book to see if any local dealers sell old records. Also check for ads that ask for records. Louis Spelicher [4350 W. Hallandale Beach Blvd., Hollywood, Florida 33023, (305) 963-5409] buys record collections.

Q. Are old transistor radios worth saving or should I dump them?
A. Don't dump them. In an article in the *Chicago Tribune*, Cara Greenburg says these transistors are collectibles. Some go for hundreds and occasionally for thousands. They originally sold for $30 to $40. Go to a few swap meets. You will have fun and get richer. They don't have to work. Collectable U.S. brands are Regency, Raytheon, Sonora, Hoffman, and Mitchell. The brightly colored models are good sellers. The U.S.-made 1954 Regency TR-1 with its large, round tuner and perforated grill sold for $2,000.

Q. What is a lacy looking cast-iron bench stamped Peter Timmes Son, Brooklyn, NY, 43" long, 19th century, American, worth?
A. About $1,100. Condition will influence the price.

Q. What are a pair of Boehm birds, mallards, in good condition, worth?
A. About $575.

Q. Is Hocking glass from the 1930s saleable?
A. Yes. This glass was made from 1931 to 1935, in green, pink, and topaz. Some had a frosted finish and some had gold or platinum edges. A covered butter dish sold for $100.

Q. Will a thimble issued for the birth of Prince William in 1983 become valuable?
A. A thimble with the faces of the new prince along with Charles and Diana is worth about $10 now. If William becomes king, even a thimble will go up in value. If there is a termination of the British monarchy, who knows what Royal collectibles might bring?

Q. Should I save old keys?
A. Sure. You might join Key Collectors International (P.O. Box 9397, Phoenix, AZ 85068). Don't discard any until you are sure you don't need them to open anything, especially small keys for boxes, drawers, trunks, etc. Also, various keys might open other locks and may come in handy. Hotel keys are becoming collectable as hotels go to plastic. Those plastic cards will probably become collectable someday too. There isn't much money to be had from selling keys right now unless they are very special. Antique keys make an interesting collection.

Q. What do you think a Flemish tapestry from the 19th century might be worth?
A. Sight unseen, this is hard to answer. Condition will affect the price. One 80" x 105" recently sold for $1,000.

Q. Do you think Victorian silverplate will increase in value?
A. Yes. It has interesting designs and its style, as well as its age, will be very appealing to future collectors. It is increasing at the moment.

Q. Is ordinary silverplate saleable?

A. Everything is saleable, however, ordinary silverplate does not inspire buyers.

Q. I have a 1940s office chair manufactured by Shaw-Walker. Do you know if it's worth anything?

A. Shaw-Walker chairs were made between 1946 and 1952 for less than $100. Today they sell between $250 and $350 for ergonomic aluminum and wood frame "Correct Seating" chairs.

Q. I have a Victorian sofa with two matching chairs. I called a local auction house who said I would not get much for them. What do you advise?

A. Contact another auction house. Also check with a Galena, Illinois, directory listing antique furniture shops where Victorian furniture sells well. New Orleans does well with Victorian pieces. Check the list of auction houses in the chapter on auctions. The pieces could also go into a house sale.

Q. What does a red tag or red dot on an item at an auction signify?

A. This means the object has been sold.

Q. I have a Baccarat paperweight with a green overlay with interlacing garlands including six silhouette canes. The sides are cut with five large round facets and with thirteen oval facets around the lower sides. The bottom is star-cut. It is French, from about 1850, and about three inches in diameter. What is it worth?

A. A like piece is on the market for $11,500.

Q. What are free collectibles?

A. This term refers to things such as fruit stickers. You just peel them off your fruit. Matchbooks from restaurants and hotels. Business cards. Luggage labels. Any unusual labels. Cereal boxes. These items are now creating unusual collections and they are all free.

Q. What new things can you think of to form a singular collection?

A. Lottery tickets maybe. How about clothing labels?

Q. I inherited a New Century music box with 15 discs. Can you give me a possible price?

A. One recently sold for $4,500. This is more than many pianos bring. Congratulations.

Q. I am thinking about collecting iron match holders. What is their price range?

A. These pieces were made in about 1860. While many were made of iron, others were made of glass, porcelain, lacquer, wood or papier-mâché. They range from about $10 up to $250. Many are from around $20 to $60.

Q. Can you tell me about kitchen collectibles?

A. Read *300 Years of Kitchen Collectibles,* a book by Linda Franklin (Books Americana), to answer your questions.

Q. Are Storybook Dolls from the 1940s collectibles?

A. Yes, many sell for over $100.

Q. Is a bear rug saleable?

A. They sell for around $400, with the head still on it.

Q. Should I save my son's sports items?

A. Sport collectibles sell great. If you have the space, I would advise saving his things. He might want them back a few years from now. Various antique shows have exhibitors offering old sports items.

Q. I found, in my grandmother's drawer, a card of bobby-pins. They are on a lady's head card. I didn't know what they were. Does anyone collect bobby-pins?

A. Yes. They sell for around $8. They were used to hold hair in place. Maybe they still do.

Q. Does anyone buy old letters by non-famous people? I have correspondence from my great-grandfather, who was a sea captain, to his brother.

A. Write or call Schmitt [P.O. Box 67, Woodbury, NY 11797, (516) 367-4030]. They buy interesting letters, diaries, journals, documents and manuscripts.

Q. Who buys automobile literature like sales brochures, owners manuals, showroom items or repair manuals?

A. Try Walter Miller [6710 Brooklawn Parkway, Syracuse, NY 13211, (315) 432-8282].

Q. Is there such a thing as a lamp dealer?

A. Yes. Danny Gipson buys lamps [7920 Potomac, Weatherby Lake, Missouri 64152, (800) 746-6048]. He also purchases vases. Wanted are: Gallé, Marinot, Decorchmont, Rousseau, Daum, Loetz, Tiffany, Daum Deco, Lalique, A. Walter, Pairpoint, Handel, Murano, B&S, Italian, Gouby, KPM, Flemish, OHR, Steuben, Webb, Burmese, Icart, Art Pottery, Frank Lloyd Wright, Thuret, Teco, Roycroft, Czech, Milano, Newcomb, All Reverse PT/Leaded Lamps. He will even pay a finder's fee.

Q. Who buys fine perfume bottles?

A. Try Monsen and Baer [Box 529, Vienna, Virginia 22183, (703) 938-2129].

Q. Is there a dealer specializing in tapestries?

A. Yes. Contact Renaté Halpern Galleries, (212) 988-9316, in New York.

Q. I have collected various prints by American artists. Is there a dealer I might contact?

A. Yes. Kenneth, Harry or Robert Newman at the Old Print Shop [150 Lexington Avenue, New York, NY 10016, (212) 683-3950]. They buy American prints by artists such as Gustave Baumann, Frank Benson, Thomas Benton, Howard

Cook, Wanda Gag, Childe Hassam, Martin Lewis, Louis Lozowick, and Wengeroth. Also, marine and naval subjects and Currier and Ives lithographs and Audubon prints.

GLOSSARY

Absentee bid
Also called a pocket bid, is an offer left in person or by mail with the auctioneer before the sale. This is kept by the auction house and is given the same recognition as bids made during the actual sale.

Appraiser
A person trained to place monetary values on property.

Apron piece
A skirt between the legs of a case piece, such as a chest or secretary.

Art glass
A term which refers to many types of glassware made during the late 19th and early 20th centuries. These pieces were always finely made and expensive, and many were made by hand.

Authentic furniture
This refers to pieces whose origin is supported by unquestionable evidence. An authentic piece will be "of the period," with proper woods and design. An authentic piece does not have to be antique. It is that which was made originally—not a copy. Many modern pieces by Herman Miller, Charles Eames or Ludwig Mies van der Rohe are authentic, but copies of these classics are not.

Base
The horizontal element on case pieces immediately above the feet.

Bentwood
Designed by Michael Thonet in the 19th century, these pieces were constructed from bent solid lengths of beechwood. They are originally from the Victorian period.

Bought-in
This is an auction term that describes what happens when a piece does not sell and is kept by the house. The piece will then go back to the owner unless other arrangements are made.

Bracket foot
A foot supporting a case piece that is attached directly to the underframing. Examples seen on Chippendale desks.

Breakfront
A cabinet having a central section, often a desk, extending forward from those on either side. It usually has glass fronted doors in the upper section and drawers or cabinets in the lower section.

Cabochon
A term used to describe the oval shape of some jewelry, buttons, leatherwork, silver, furniture, etc. Raised oval ornaments, usually carved, were used for furniture decoration.

Castor
A small wheel on a swivel attached to furniture legs. Examples seen on American Sheraton chairs.

Chinoiserie
This refers to an 18th-century style of decoration in which supposedly Chinese motifs were used. We see this form of decoration from the 18th century to the present—usually with gold decoration on black or vermillion lacquer.

Country furniture
This is furniture made in rural communities of local woods, often primitive, but employing basic designs from urban areas.

Country pieces from Europe are often called provincial pieces, meaning they were made in the provinces.

Crotch-grain
This term describes veneer generally cut from the main crotch or fork of a tree.

Cupboard
This term usually means a cabinet for food or clothing. In America we often call the clothing type of cupboard a wardrobe while in France it is called an armoire.

Depression glass
An inexpensive glass manufactured by many American glass factories during the 1920s in a variety of colors and patterns.

Dovetails
Devices used to fasten wood together by fitting wedge-shaped or dovetail-shaped pieces into corresponding negative spaces. Examples are often seen on drawers.

Escutcheon
A shield-shaped piece that covers the keyhole. Can be made of wood, ivory or metal. This is also referred to as a mount.

Extension table
A table which opens from the center and moves in both directions in order to make room for loose leaves in the open part.

Fiddle-back
A fiddle-shaped splat found on chairs. A narrow fiddle shape may be called a spoon-back.

Finial
A decorative ornament that points up or down.

Figures
Timber designs brought out by cutting the wood so surfaces

display various types of irregularities in the grain and color.

Fly-rail
The swinging bracket which supports a drop leaf.

French polishing
This term means shellacked with a glass-like finish. It is flashier than a natural patina.

Georgian
The English period from the accession of George I in 1714 to the death of George IV in 1830.

In the style of
A term that refers to pieces made to resemble the workmanship of an earlier period. For example, an "in the style of" Chippendale chest may have been made in the 20th century, while an original would have been made in the 18th century.

Inlay
Inserting wood of a contrasting color or texture into the surface of a piece for decoration. When inlay is done in straight lines, it is called stringing. Brass is also considered an inlay material.

Lowboy
This term usually refers to a low, table-like chest, inspired by the English flat-topped dressing table.

Market value
The retail cash value of a piece.

Marquetry
Contrasts inlay. It can be woods combined with tortoise shell, brass, or mother-of-pearl.

Natural patina
This is the furniture surface which, if left untreated, will be even in color and have a mellow quality. Furniture with original

patinas are greatly appreciated. Poorly restored pieces will appear harsh compared to naturally aged pieces. One of the reasons people treasure old furniture is for their soft color hues.

Ormolu
Gilded bronze, brass, or copper mounts. Associated with French furniture, it is also seen on other Continental and English pieces.

Papier-mâché
Molded paper pulp that was used for many furniture pieces in the Victorian and Napoleon III periods. It was suitable for japaning and polishing. Various pieces were inlaid with mother-of-pearl and were also painted with added decorations. By the 1860s this form of decoration was outmoded.

Paquetry
This refers to inlay executed in geometric patterns.

Rail
A horizontal, connecting piece in furniture construction. Chairs have seat-rails, crest-rails, and back-rails. A rail holds the sides of case pieces together.

Reproduction
A copy. Some furniture copies are a hundred years old and some are new.

Reserved auction
When the minimum bid for each piece is determined by the auction house, the auction is reserved. In an unreserved auction the piece always goes to the highest bidder—no matter how low the bid may be.

Restoration
This is more than a simple repair. It means to renew and return a piece to its original state. New parts can be substituted for

missing or damaged ones. Without restoration beautiful pieces would be lost.

Revivals
Designs and styles from previous time periods.

Stretcher
The crosspiece which connects and braces furniture legs. Stretchers may be curved, flat, carved, or made of metal.

Unreserved auction
An auction in which a piece goes for the highest bid, however low it may be. A good way to buy, a poor way to sell.

Veneer
A separate layer of wood that is applied to the base wood. Sometimes called a furniture skin, veneer was used in ancient Egypt and is still used today.

BIBLIOGRAPHY

Ad Age, (January 1995).

Ad Age, (April 1995).

Art and Antiques, (October 1994): 70–72.

Art and Auction, (January 1995): 107–118.

Art and Auction, (February 1995).

Kovels on Antiques and Collectibles, vol. 18, no. 6, (February 1992): 71.

Kovels on Antiques and Collectibles, vol. 18, no. 10, (June 1992): 111.

Kovels on Antiques and Collectibles, vol. 19, no. 1, (September 1992): 11.

Kovels on Antiques and Collectibles, vol. 19, no. 10, (June 1993): 115.

Kovels on Antiques and Collectibles, vol. 19, no. 11, (July 1993): 21, 126.

Kovels on Antiques and Collectibles, vol. 19, no. 12, (August 1993): 135.

Kovels on Antiques and Collectibles, vol. 20, no. 2, (October 1993).

Kovels on Antiques and Collectibles, vol. 20, no. 10, (June 1994): 120.

Kovels on Antiques and Collectibles, vol. 20, no. 11, (July 1994): 131.

Kovels Newsletter, (January 1992): 51, 53.

Leckey, Andrew. "Personal Finance." *Chicago Tribune*, Section 6 (December 1994): 8.

Lewis, Peter. "Auction on the Internet." *The New York Times* (May 1995).

Maine Antique Digest, The, (August 1994): 37A.

Maine Antique Digest, The, (January 1995): 13–21.

Maine Antique Digest, The, (February 1995).

Maine Antique Digest, The, (March 1995): 6A, 26B, 34–35C, 40C, 1–3D, 19E, 41G.

Maine Antique Digest, The, (May 1995): 3B, 36–37C, 12–14D, 32D, 43D, 13E, 32E, 3F.

Mateja, Jim. "Used Cars." *Chicago Tribune* (September 1994).

Ritter, Don. *Whole Earth Online Almanac from A to Z.* Brody, New York, 1993.

Schiffer, Nancy and Herbert. *Woods We Live With.* Schiffer Limited, 1977.

Siegel, Jeanne. *How to Speak Furniture with an Antique English Accent.* Bonus Books, Chicago, 1992.

Siegel, Jeanne. *How to Speak Furniture with an Antique French Accent.* Bonus Books, Chicago, 1994.

Siegel, Jeanne. *How to Speak Furniture with an Antique Victorian Accent.* Bonus Books, Chicago, 1991.

Smith, Michael. "Your Money." *Chicago Tribune* (October 1994).

World Book Encyclopedia, The, vol. 15 (1992): 203.

INDEX

ABOUT THE AUTHOR

Jeanne Siegel is a residential contents appraiser and the author of four other books: *How to Speak Furniture with an Antique American Accent, How to Speak Furniture with an Antique Victorian Accent, How to Speak Furniture with an Antique English Accent* and *How to Speak Furniture with an Antique French Accent.* She also teaches Buying and Selling Antiques at Oakton Community College.

Everyone can make good money selling their possessions intelligently. How to sell intelligently is what this book is about.